SOMEHOW
A Miracle of Spiritual Birth

SOMEHOW
A Miracle of Spiritual Birth

by
Darko Velichkovski

QUAIL RIDGE PRESS

Published by
QUAIL RIDGE PRESS
P. O. Box 123 • Brandon, MS 39043 • 1-800-343-1583
info@quailridge.com • www.quailridge.com

Manufactured in the United States of America
Front cover photo by Karla Pound
Design by Barney McKee

Library of Congress Cataloging-in-Publication Data

Velichkovski, Darko
Somehow : a miracle of spiritual birth / by Darko Velichkovski.
p. cm.
ISBN 1-893062-68-6
1. Velichkovski, Darko 2. Conversion—Christianity. 3. Christian biography. I. Title.

BV4935.V45A3 2004
248.2'46'092—dc22   2004020138

ISBN 1-893062-68-6

10 9 8 7 6 5 4 3 2 1

First Edition

In Memory
of
Mr. Stuart C. Irby, Jr.

God has blessed me immeasurably by bringing you into my life,
even if for just a few short years. You were the closest
I ever had to a grandfather, and I am eternally grateful for all the
wisdom, friendship and Christ-like love you so selflessly shared
with me. Your heart, your mind and your soul have
left an indelible imprint onto my life, and I will never be the same
because of it. I can't wait to catch up with you in
Heaven and hear you play your trumpet again.

Until then...You are the spirit of America.
You are the spirit of Christ.
May God grant me a favor to remember you long and well.

Thank you, Mr. Irby.

SOMEHOW

I

THE youth symphony orchestra practice ended promptly at noon that Sunday. As always, we rushed to our favorite café, just around a corner from the rehearsal hall. We had no real reason to rush, mind you, except that rushing increased the chances of someone's tripping on a music stand, falling down the stairs, or running into someone else, with a possible benefit of getting the best chair at the table if one makes it to the café first. But somehow, those were all good enough reasons for us to hurry even more.

As we approached, though, a worker was posting a handwritten sign on the café's door—"Closed For Renovation." All the elbowing, laughing, pushing, and pulling stopped, and we froze like a pack of deer caught in the headlights. Closed? As in "keep out," as in "no one allowed in," as in "what do we do now?" Yep. Not only closed—locked shut for an undeterminable amount of time. Tragedy in the making, indeed, with all the predictable feelings attached: first, denial; then outrage and sadness; then a sense of betrayal; and finally, panic.

And you thought only death in the family could bring out such a cycle of emotions. Well, you live and you learn. Teenagers feel things pretty deeply, warranted or not, and we were no exception. Besides, as you can clearly see, we took our café choices very seriously.

Hurriedly, we walked five blocks to the coffee shop that, although not exactly to our liking, had to suffice. "Desperate times call for desperate measures," someone said, and we all wholeheartedly agreed, settling around a table, carefully placing our instrument cases next to the wall.

As always, we emptied our pockets and put the contents all in one pile, separating coins and bills from bubble gum, candies, old concert tickets, pocketknives, bus passes, keys... And then, as if on cue, it was on to the serious business of adding up the money and checking the menu to see how many sodas and coffees we could get for it.

Since coffee was always the cheapest item on the menu, we usually had enough to order at least one each, but this time some of us had to share a cup. Obviously, somebody's parents were beginning to catch on to the magic of the "disappearing grocery change" game.

In reality, they likely couldn't afford to continue pretending. Even with the commercial and social advantages that Belgrade, the Yugoslavian capital city where we all lived, offered over the rest of the country, most of our middle class parents made only $30-50 a month. Quite simply they couldn't regard even leftover grocery change lightly.

Belgrade, Yugoslavia

So what's a teen to do? Keep taking the change, and the last week of a month your mother would send you from neighbor to neighbor, borrowing oil and eggs. Don't take the change, and you are bound to be sharing a cup of coffee with someone who will mockingly question your adulthood, manhood, and maturity, since you couldn't put together enough coins even for a coffee. Decisions, decisions.

But coffees and sodas were just backdrops, mere stage props for this ritual, and we would never have allowed such a trifling thing as sharing a cup spoil the fun. There was much more to it than just sitting around the table mindlessly consuming time and caffeinated liquids.

On the one hand, it was a by-product of a centuries-old way of life in southern Europe. Deep-rooted traditions stressed the immense importance of social and emotional investment in family, community, and friends. These interactions far transcended casual communal relationships and social norms.

We had learned it, time and time again, on those late evenings when, as children, pretending to sleep, we listened in from under a blanket to our parents, grandparents and neighbors as they shared that last pot of coffee for the day. As the generations before them had done, and as we were doing that Sunday afternoon. To share our innermost fears and hopes, to spill our souls on the table like loose change for all to pick through, to spend a few hours in each other's shoes and grow together was as important, natural, and life sustaining as breathing.

On the other hand, these gatherings had to do with the way we were taught to think of the world, our futures and ourselves. Social bonds and intellectual power were the keys to progress and desirable social status, everyone told us repeatedly. To acquire it and build it into a priceless treasure, you indeed need others—parents, neighbors, teachers, friends... Just as you need them when you run out of money for oil and eggs because the grocery change keeps disappearing, you need them to grow socially and intellectually.

And not simply to chew on their thoughts and then spit them out, which would go against all our cultural instincts. We needed rather to squeeze out and share every last ounce of our own being, to exchange ideas, to challenge and be challenged, to open up and expand our horizons, to continually learn and therefore grow.

That's how you acquire the power to mold your destiny and shape your future—by constantly enlarging the intellectual potential within you. That's where your true power as a human being lies, and where your only salvation is, the lesson said. And most of us took it seriously. Very seriously. My family certainly did.

II

WHEN I was seven years old, to supplement my general education and start broadening my cultural appreciation and horizons, my parents thought it would be a good idea for me to attend one of the local elementary music schools. They did not simply intend for me to learn how to play an instrument, but wanted me to be wholly involved in artistic learning for at least a few of those formative years. Our music school system was just the place for such an experience.

Expenses, which would normally be the first consideration, given our meager financial means, were in this case of no consideration, since all educational institutions and programs in Yugoslavia, music schools included, were free. Of course, unlike the elementary academic schools, elementary music schools admitted students based on the results of admission tests. So my parents registered me for the admission auditions, and one morning off we went to get my musical abilities and affinities probed.

After a few hours of waiting in lines, clapping, tapping and singing for various juries, I was told that I passed and that the committee needed to know my instrument preference in order to complete my registration process. "Trumpet," I said, "I want to play a

Darko, age 3

trumpet." (Loud and shiny. Surely you can see the attraction.) The teachers on the committee looked at each other for a second, and then broke into laughter.

"You are too young for a trumpet, son," one of them said, shaking his head. "You have to be at least 13 to play a trumpet. But, come here, let me take a better look at you." I came closer, and after examining my fingers, mouth and teeth, he calmly said: "You should play a clarinet. You are made for it. How about that? How about a clarinet?"

A cla-what? If it's not loud and shiny, and you can't play it on a galloping horse leading an army behind you with it, I don't think I want it, I thought. But of course, being a seven-year-old, I lowered my head, shrugged my shoulders, and drawing an invisible circle on the floor with the tip of my shoe, said: "I guess."

Soon, the first clarinet lessons and various music classes came, and I felt increasingly a part of something very special. It was as if somebody suddenly led me through a hidden gate, and whispered into my ear: "Come, let me show you something—the enchanted kingdom of music. Here, you make the stories, and tell the stories created by those who came before you.

They live through you and you walk with them, no matter how much space and time separate you. Here, everything is possible, and everyone can be a prince." And who would mind

Darko (10 years old) practicing at his desk in Belgrade, Yugoslavia. In the foreground, Darko's younger brother, Davor, looks at the camera.

missing a few play dates, a soccer game here and there, or sleep a little less for that? I didn't. I didn't mind at all.

Strange scribbles, dots and lines on the music paper slowly became familiar, discernible symbols that moved my fingers up and down my instrument, as if by magic. Bit by bit, one by one, the stories created by the long-gone princes and princesses of this kingdom came pouring out under my fingertips, tickling corners of my mind I didn't even know existed. Simple stories, at first, but to me beautiful nevertheless. No words, no pictures, yet more vivid and alive than any book or a movie I had ever seen. Enchanted kingdom, indeed.

Spending afternoons and evenings attending music

theory, ear-training, music history or harmony classes, and rehearsing with other students in orchestral and chamber music ensembles became my new routine. The music school, slowly and almost inconspicuously, came to be my home away from home, my other family; every teacher, my parent, and every student, my sibling.

By the time I was 10, music and my instrument grew so deeply under my skin that I couldn't go a day without them. Through music I could say things my words could not possibly describe. I could speak to hundreds or thousands at one time, through that miraculous language that had no censors, no limits, and needed no translation. What a power! What a joy! Intoxicating, to say the least, especially to a 10-year-old.

Darko (13 years old), his parents, and his brother in their apartment in Belgrade, Yugoslavia.

III

I KNEW then that music would become a lifelong commitment. My parents lovingly supported this newfound passion of mine, but warned me that their support would last only as long as my other academic endeavors didn't suffer because of it. Semester after semester, with my high grades and scholastic honors, I continually assured them that I had no intention of neglecting academics, and that I knew that life wasn't all about music. I indeed understood how important academic accomplishment was for my future, as well.

Very early on, I learned that my heroes should be those who lived through hundreds of thousands of pages of literature, poetry, science, music, and philosophy they created. To make something of myself, to one day be somebody, I needed to catch every subtle move of their minds and soak in every drop of their wisdom. Plato, Aristotle, Sophocles, Cicero, Thucydides, Boethius, Voltaire, Hume, Rousseau... I needed their strong, wide shoulders to anchor the foundation of my future.

And then there were those sacred political giants and icons of the communist world whose thoughts and works were written in pen, as well as in blood. I was told not only to study them diligently, but more importantly, to revere their sheer genius, courage, and revolutionary vision. They gave us the freedom and security we were enjoying all over eastern Europe—freedom from the capitalist exploiters, freedom from the bloodthirsty royalties, freedom from the shackles of religion, superstition, and ignorance.

Marx and Engels sowed this freedom's seed through their 1848 Communist Manifesto. Lenin and Trotsky watered it to its first sprout as they led the 1917 Bolshevik Revolution. Finally this freedom came to our country in all the beauty of its full blossom at the end of WWII in 1945.

Over a thousand years of Christianity and its traditions in this part of the Balkans ended as Roosevelt, Churchill and Stalin, in their collective wisdom, handed the reins of the Kingdom of Yugoslavia over to Marshal Tito, his partisans, and the Communist Party.

The new government renamed the country the Socialist Federal Republic of Yugoslavia. They dealt with the many remains of its Christian history, monarchial politics and capitalist past brutally and swiftly. Our glorious Party, after decades of superhuman struggles on behalf of the people, had finally won the ultimate, long coveted prize—absolute power.

True, hundreds of thousands, perhaps millions, of Yugoslavians either had to die or be permanently imprisoned to clean the slate and make the break

Marshal Tito playing both sides ...

... *with Brezhnew*

... *with Khrushchev*

... *with Kim Il Sung*

... *with Fidel Castro*

... *with Ho Shi Minh*

... with Jimmy Carter

... with Winston Churchill

... with Richard Nixon

... with John F. Kennedy

from the past complete. But that was understandable, the Party contended. A thousand years of grime don't wash off easily.

Where the water and soap of political propaganda and indoctrination didn't work, the heavy wire brushes of the secret police—their sticks, prisons and bullets—were sure to scrub it clean. The Party needed a wholly clean slate on which to etch the great truths denied to us for centuries. We, the people, needed enlightenment and the Party was there to lead us bravely to it. Long live the Communist Party!

IV

THE enlightenment came and swept through the nation like a monumental flood—a flood of political, educational, economic and social reforms and decrees.

The Soviet and Chinese governments set a shining example for our new country, as those who paved the way toward the ultimate victory of communism. Our fearless leader, the father of our new nation, the one to whom we owed and pledged our very lives, Marshal Josip Broz Tito, was installed first as the prime minister, and then as the president of the country, the commander-in-chief of the armed forces, and the secretary general of the Communist Party of Yugoslavia, for life.

His portraits and murals sprang up on the walls of every public building and square. Like thick smoke seeping in through the cracks, they quickly found their way into living rooms, dorms, and lockers. Just as with his early role models, Stalin and Mao, the magic dust of the Communist Revolution transformed every word he spoke into a breath of life, every decree into a bright path, and every book, prepared in his name by his writers, into a glorious monument of progress.

Children all over the country memorized his life and thoughts, quoting him just as easily and naturally at the dinner table as in the classroom. With Tito in their hearts and the Party on their minds, the new Yugoslavian youth made the future of communism in our country look bright.

The Party leadership could now mold and shape that seemingly unlimited supply of fresh, unspoiled human material to their content. And they have indeed painstakingly done so.

They wrote new history books—for the past had to be skillfully edited for young and innocent minds to digest. They wrote new curricula—for, it was obvious to them that the old Yugoslavian education system, with its inclusion of Christian theology and capitalist economics and its total disregard for Marxist theories and socialism, resulted in gross intellectual corruption of its students. They hired new school administrators—for surely our young, bright, Soviet-educated, card-carrying members of the Communist Party would do a better job managing schools than their morally corrupt, western-leaning, bourgeois predecessors.

So began the ceaseless effort to capture, and permanently alter, the hearts and the minds of Yugoslavian youth.

V

S I M U L T A N E O U S L Y, the Communist Party had a unique way of dealing with organized religion in the country. In Yugoslavia, unlike in the other communist countries around the world, going to church or declaring oneself a Christian wasn't illegal, but simply socially unacceptable, shameful, and irrational.

Instead of overt physical persecution of Christians, which would most likely have resulted in an active underground Church, as in the Soviet Union and Romania, the Yugoslavian Communist Party opted for slower, but ultimately much more cunning and thorough, eradication of the Church from its midst.

Our Party ideologues and leaders knew that although they had to deal violently with the immediate threat of the unwavering and unrepentant Church leadership, there was no reason to violently annihilate entire congregations as well and risk a potentially devastating political PR fiasco. The number of the faithful, having already been drastically reduced by the lack of leadership, would significantly decrease even further with each new generation, they reasoned, if they created the "appropriate" social, professional, and intellectual environments throughout the country.

First, they established a system of education based

on the spiritually lethal mixture of humanism and socialism. After the Party's educational arm was through with them, students had atheism set so deeply in their minds that it became the only acceptable and logical view of the world—the definitive sign of human progress and the ultimate product of the intellectual evolution of mankind.

Second, the universal requirement of Party membership for all but the most menial jobs meant that a Christian had to choose between being able to provide adequately for his family and living on the very edge of existence. The extreme hardship of life without the "red ID" led many believers into Party membership, which forced them to sever all ties to the Christian community, further depleting its numbers and strength. To make things even more difficult, a Party member could be severely punished if he or she was found to propagate religion, even within the family circle. Such tactics made the age-old practice of generational transfer of Christian spiritual values an extremely dangerous and, therefore, very rare, activity.

Third, and most important, every possible public sign of affirmation of the Christian ideology was methodically and painstakingly removed, replaced with secular and humanist counterparts. Newspapers, magazines, television, radio, music, film, art, literature became void of any traces of religion, especially Christianity and its spiritual tenets.

On those rare occasions when it did appear in the

media, literature or curricula, it was either mocked, studied strictly academically (and always along with other world religions in order to equalize its beliefs with the other figments of spiritual imagination around the world), or wondered at as some deformed monstrosity. (Some of the centuries-old churches and monasteries were spared, however, to be used predominately as museums, where tourists and students could study their architecture, frescoes and mosaics as curious remnants of our "admittedly ignorant, but artistically creative past," as our teachers would put it.)

My parents were among the first generation to be targeted by that effort. As a teenager, my mother received a government scholarship to attend a boarding high school in Zagreb, the capital of the Yugoslavian republic of Croatia. Consequently, she left her family and her birthplace on the Adriatic coast of Dalmatia in early 1950s and spent the rest of her school years at the communist–run boarding school. Since her father was killed in World War II and her mother left alone to provide for three children, this scholarship ensured not only my mother's education, but also a better chance of survival for the rest of the family, which now had one less mouth to feed. Eventually, my mother worked her way up to become an executive in the government–run textile production industry.

My father lost both of his parents in World War II. His uncle's family, who lived in a sheep-raising village in the mountains of Macedonia, adopted him. Most village children had to drop out of school after a few years of elementary education and begin tending sheep full time in order to survive. My father was no exception.

But spending his life as a shepherd was just not meant to be. In a torn piece of a newspaper he retrieved from the garbage one day, he read an article describing an educational program the Army was setting up in Macedonia. They were recruiting the brightest children from all over the country and offered them a free education, which was to take them all the way through the military academies. Overwhelmed by the promise of an education and a better future, my father ran away from his adopted home and spent the rest of his youth in the military schools. Ultimately, he became an officer in the Yugoslavian Air Force.

Both of my parents, like millions of Yugoslavians at the time, were raised by the Communist Party and its ideologies. They were our country's future, and the Party leaders carefully and determinedly fed them a steady diet of Marxism, Leninism, Titoism and atheism throughout their education. Even had they been aware of the deliberate caging of their minds and souls, they would not have had a chance of fighting off such an overwhelming force bearing down on them. The mold was set, and they were going to fit in it, one way or another. The Party would see to it.

VI

O F course, growing up, neither I nor any of my friends was aware of any of these deliberate efforts to destroy our country's Christian spiritual legacy and steer the Yugoslavian people as far from it as possible. We simply didn't feel spiritually or intellectually deprived. Nothing around us contradicted the atheistic worldview we learned from our parents and teachers. As a matter of fact, everywhere we looked, we saw nothing but confirmation of its truths.

As first graders, one glorious morning, the morning impatiently anticipated for years, with great pomp and celebration by our whole community—our parents, teachers, neighbors, and political leaders—we were inducted into the ranks of Tito's Pioneers. Dressed in white shirts, red bandanas around our necks, and each wearing a blue communist partisan-style hat with a red five-point star sewn on its front, we stood tall and proud, soaking in the communist wisdom imparted on us that day by one of the regional Party leaders at our local elementary school auditorium.

He spoke of the fruits of our country's glorious communist revolution and the imperative to preserve and grow that precious harvest. Those red bandanas around our necks were the reminders of the blood spilled for our freedom from the capitalist exploiters, he told us. Our white shirts were to remind us to remain pure in our devotion, commitment and faithfulness to the leadership of the Party and the wisdom of our dearest comrade—Marshal Tito.

The blue hats, he implored us to always remember, represented our sky, free from superstitions, saints, angels, and God, free from all the religious and spiritual enslavers of our minds. And that red star sewn on each hat was the bright light illuminating our path, lovingly and sacrificially paved for us by the communists who came before us. For, it was our turn now to walk that path and carry the righteous burden of the revolution, and we needed as much red illumination as possible, he exclaimed.

One day we were playing in the mud, and the next, we were dressed in crisp Pioneers' uniforms, asked to carry "the righteous burden of the revolution." I remember thinking: "I bet we'll get nice red backpacks to carry the 'burden' in. Maybe even a gun to protect it from the capitalists and the fascists. That would be really cool. They already gave us these nice uniforms…"

The years that followed were filled with classes sprinkled with socialist and atheist doctrines, saluting at army parades, walking in celebration marches, red flag-waving at black limousines driving through the

Wearing their government issued uniforms, first grade students celebrate induction into the ranks of Tito's Pioneers.

squares, and occasional faintings at the communist holiday ceremonial speech gatherings. And for all of it we got a pat on the back from our parents and praise from the Party leaders. But the brainwashing didn't end there.

We turned on our TV sets and watched programs sanctioned by the government; programs like Carl Sagan's Cosmos, for example. Remember Sagan? "The cosmos is the only thing that ever was, is and always will be," he liked to say, with all the drama and the chip on the shoulder of a true spiritual midget.

And how can one forget the celebrated nighttime soaps, Peyton Place and Dynasty? All the opulence, intrigue, exploitation and excess of the West we were taught to despise, yet so delicious to watch. Can you think of any shows more fitting than these for social-ist television programming?

We read newspapers owned by the government, attended plays approved by the government, studied curricula created by the government. Everything we ever heard and saw was carefully placed in our midst by the government, and yet we never caught on.

Actually, every once in a while we would hear of someone who did catch on and revolted, especially among my parents' and grandparents' generations, but it was always those with "questionable character, shady reputation, unstable personality, and antisocial tendencies"... or at least that's what the TV newscasts said. Why should we question it? If it was on the news, it must be true. Of course, the Party had a way with these characters. As far as we were told, they were urgently needed in their professional capacities, and sent away on "business trips"... for life.

Unlike some of the previous generations, though, those who still remembered the former freedoms of our Christian, capitalist, and monarchial past, most of my generation was completely oblivious to the brainwashing to which it was subjected, and played along, not only willingly, but enthusiastically. The world presented to us by the Party, by our teachers and parents, was the only world we knew, and we readily embraced it, with all of its apparent political, economic and intellectual schizophrenia.

Schizophrenia? Yes. Just consider the following:

• On the one hand, we were the "People's Republic," the land of freedom and liberty; and on the other, we suffered under a dictatorship.

• On the one hand we lived from hand to mouth; and on the other, we enjoyed annual month-long summer vacations on the coast, and skied in the mountains for weeks every winter. (To keep the workers from revolting because of the low wages, the government made domestic travel and tourism very affordable, mandatory vacation days abundant, and personal loans readily available. Inventive, isn't it?)

• On the one hand we were to strive for intellectual excellence; and on the other, our very minds were sacrificed to the gods of atheism, humanism and materialism.

As I said—political, economic, and intellectual schizophrenia, which my generation didn't, and couldn't, see as anomaly, but as the norm.

So far as we were concerned, life in Yugoslavia wasn't that bad. Sure, we wanted to have larger allowances, less homework, longer hair, finer clothes, nicer cars, better stereos... but, that's just teenagers being teenagers. We still had our concerts, tours, museums, libraries, theaters, cafés, and, of course, each other.

VII

"EIGHT coffees and a pitcher of water, please."
Our waiter took a quick look at us and softly
sighed, shaking his head and rolling his eyes in disap-
pointment. Who could blame him? Considering our
"generous" order, which we were dividing amongst a
dozen of us, the tip was bound to be just as generous.
Not that he worked for tips, but every little extra was
cherished.

It took an unusually long time for our order to
arrive, but we knew better than to complain. We
were lucky to get it at all. The waiter could have simply refused to notice us, much less to serve us. But, as
I said, we were lucky that day.

For, here, unlike in the West, customer satisfaction
didn't mean much. Neither the security of one's job
nor one's salary depended on it. In addition, neither
was based on the quantity one produced, the quality
of the service one provided, the complexity of one's
work, or the extent of one's education and experience. So what was it based on? Well, that's a more
complex question than you can imagine, and you
might regret asking it.

All the businesses in the new socialist Yugoslavia

belonged to the government and were, therefore, run by the government. Theoretically, the government was "of the people, for the people" (sound familiar?), but with a uniquely communist twist: to be "the people," one had to be a member of the Party.

This fact, of course, meant that only proven Party loyalists managed all the businesses, which, in turn, meant that to get hired for all but the most menial jobs, one also had to be a member of the Party. The Party ran the whole show; and one was either in or out. And believe me, one could not afford to be out.

The management mechanism of choice was the workers' committee. Headed by the business' general manager, as well as by the career Party functionary, it was composed of workers chosen by their peers. Since all the internal management decisions, including personnel issues, were made at this level, dismissing a worker based on his performance became a relic of our shameful capitalist past. On the other hand, firing a worker based on his weakening loyalty to the Party, or his questionable respect and devotion to the visionary leadership of our Marshal Tito was, of course, a different story.

The government's economic planning committees largely set the workers' salary scales on the national level. These scales were based on a number of determining factors, none of which even resembled the basic principles of scientific economy. Since production quotas and actual profits were taken out of the equation, the government relied on foreign loans to keep the system afloat.

The government adhered to the communist principle of aiming for a classless society, though, and workers' salaries were set only a small fraction apart, regardless of the industry, its complexity or its actual contribution to the overall economy. This system, coupled with the fact that most of the salary levels were just barely enough to survive, virtually eliminated the distinction between the middle and lower classes in society. The communist reasoning was that if everyone had to spend most of their income on bread, milk, oil and eggs, with a minimal opportunity for the accumulation of personal savings and "nest eggs," the bliss of social and economic equality was sure to follow. Brilliant, isn't it?

And what about the upper class? Well, that's a touchy subject. Officially, there was no "upper class." But as much as the Party leaders preached about the virtues of the classless society, they themselves were economically and socially separated from "the people." The higher they were in the political hierarchy, the more opulent their financial and social benefits. Limos, villas, spas, butlers, bodyguards...all of it, you understand, just the necessary tools so our esteemed leaders could carry on their important work on behalf of us all.

We, "the people," of course, knew that one day we

would all be equal, for the Party told us so. But for now, the Party leaders were willing to sacrifice their own personal purity, for as long as necessary, and take on the burden of those admittedly tasteless and painful capitalist habits of luxury and privilege to complete the work of the revolution and help us all reach that glorious communist ideal of equality. How noble. How selfless. How distinctly communist.

VIII

BY the time our coffees arrived, we had already dissected every note of the previous night's Belgrade Philharmonic performance, exchanged a few choruses of "Have you heard..." and "Can you believe..." and were beginning to take sides in the always popular, yet dangerously passionate, discussion of the Nietzsche-Wagner connection. Predictably, someone brought up Hitler, his reverence for Wagner's music and Nietzsche's philosophy, and the disastrous consequences of German nationalism.

Darko (16 years old), second from left, with a group of students in Cavtat, Monte Negro, after a performance.

The artistic purists among us were crying foul and doing their best to blow up the bridges between politics and music. Just as our debate turned from stimulating to nauseating, the door to the coffee shop swung open. A man slowly entered and approached the pastry counter; not just an ordinary man, but someone whose very appearance seemed to scream: "I am not from around here! Not from this town, not from this country, not even from this continent!"

And then he said a few words to the waiter and we instantly knew—an American tourist...in person, in all his glory. Wagner and Nietzsche just couldn't compete and we instantly dumped them for our new interest.

With the quiet awe of birdwatchers caught off-guard by a rare species, we silently observed this human phenomenon: safari hat, several layers of mismatched shirts, blue jeans, worn-out sneakers, leather back-pocket-wallet chained to a belt, shoulder-strapped video camera, and of course, a super automatic photo camera around the neck.

"Maybe we should try talking to him," I whispered.

Silence.

"The waiter can't understand a thing this guy is saying. Maybe we can help him order. Among us all, we know at least that much English," I said a little louder.

Silence. All eyes still on the tourist.

At that moment, obviously frustrated by his inability to order, he turned around, looked straight at me, and said: "Do you, by any chance, speak English?"

"A little," I said, at which the rest of the group suddenly joined in, affirming our collective familiarity with his language, however basic.

We asked him to join us at our table, helped him with his order, and spent the next hour or so visiting and practicing our English language skills. His name was Kelley Travis, and he was a retired attorney from Jackson, Mississippi, currently enjoying his retirement by traveling around the world. As he was going to be in Belgrade for a few more days, we offered to show him around.

He gratefully accepted, and we quickly drew a plan of tours and schedules on a napkin. Everyone around the table picked a few two-hour shifts, and for the next 48 hours we became "Mister Kelley's tour guides," touting the beauty, history and cultural riches of our city like experienced car salesmen showing off their newest models.

My last shift coincided with his last few hours in Belgrade, and I was to help him check out of his hotel as well as make sure that he got on the right bus for the airport. About an hour before the bus departed, over our last cup of coffee in his hotel's restaurant, Mr. Travis told me that he wanted something other than the usual souvenirs to remember his visit by. He asked me if, by any chance, I could give him a tape of one of my performances as a memento.

Since Belgrade's main radio station facilities were close by, and they had just recently broadcasted one of my solo performances as part of their National Young Musicians Competition Winners series, I called the program director and asked for a copy of the broadcast. An hour later, Mr. Travis boarded the airport bus—safari hat, cameras and all—his luggage by his side, and the cassette tape memento in his pocket.

In a few weeks he won't even remember our names, and Belgrade will become just a blur in his memory, I thought, not lamenting, but simply affirming the fact. And that was understandable, for we were but a few among hundreds he met on his journey around the world. He couldn't possibly keep up with all the names and places. Little did I know that this brief, accidental encounter with an American tourist and that tape he now carried in his pocket would eventually change my life forever.

IX

THE "Mister Kelley Affair" slowly faded from our minds, and life returned to its normal flow. For me and most of my friends, it was back to rehearsals, concerts, books, exams, and late nights in Belgrade cafés.

I was 16 years old, one of the youngest undergraduate students at the University of Belgrade's Music Conservatory, four-time consecutive winner of the National Young Musicians Competition, and principal clarinetist and soloist of the Belgrade Youth Philharmonic. By this time, my youthful fascination with music had become an overwhelming passion for that art and my instrument, resulting in an irreversible decision to spend the rest of my life in pursuit of that most elusive of all musical goals—artistic perfection.

Every Sunday morning and Wednesday evening, my friends and I would rehearse with the Belgrade Youth Philharmonic, religiously. (Pun intended. For those not familiar with Christian worship schedules, Sunday mornings and, in the Protestant tradition, Wednesday evenings, as well, are when Christians gather for their worship services. What a coincidence that those are the exact days and hours at which our Youth Philharmonic rehearsals took place.)

That musical ensemble, sponsored by the government, consisted of about 80 of the best music high school and conservatory students. We performed standard symphonic repertoire throughout the year, traveling all over the country and Europe—France, Switzerland, Austria, Italy... And we loved it and enjoyed it all immensely.

What was there not to love? We were only teenagers, but already devoted to music and artistic excellence for life, knowing what we needed and wanted to do, and doing it—practicing, rehearsing, performing, recording, competing, touring. We were not merely allowed to do it, mind you, but enabled, encouraged, and praised for it. A teenager's dream, don't you think? To do the thing you love the most, and not get in trouble—a pure adolescent utopia.

Academically, as I mentioned earlier, most of us strived for excellence as well. Naturally, some of us were more inclined and persistent than others, but we didn't dispute the fact that wide general knowledge and broad intellectual betterment mattered. Rarely would you hear the grudging argument, so often heard among students in the West, that once you have chosen your major and decided on your future profession, a serious study of unrelated academics becomes irrelevant and, therefore, unnecessary.

Some of us might have been too lazy to pursue it, some of us might not have known how to manage time well and have fallen behind, some of us might not have had a natural disposition for certain subjects, but all of us were absolutely convinced of the immense intrinsic value of human knowledge. In our own ways, and according to our abilities and affinities, we all worshiped it.

The lessons I had learned from my parents and teachers about the importance of constantly striving to better oneself academically had remained deeply etched on my mind, and I continued to pore over thousands of pages of history, literature, science and poetry. Some of it was for my academic courses at the conservatory, and some for my own enjoyment.

X

MY most preferred extracurricular interest was philosophy. The study began to occupy my mind when I first encountered the works and thoughts of Plato and Aristotle in my elementary school history and literature classes. Through my initial surface readings of Plato I got my first "accredited" philosophical confirmation of what my parents, teachers and government taught me to believe since I was born.

To discover the nature of "the good," and to achieve "the good life," Plato maintained that one must acquire knowledge—knowledge that is ascertainable and accessible only through the human faculties of reason and mental discipline. For those not versed in the basics of Plato's ethical theories, "the good life" is not equivalent to this phrase's modern connotation of "party all the time," but is the life based on knowing what is right, leading to the eradication of evil. He believed that to attain this knowledge and to build one's mental capacity necessary for appropriately processing it so it can lead to "the good life," one must undergo a long period of intellectual training.

So contrary to our popular teenage opinion, in

addition to my parents and teachers, even Plato thought that the amount of homework assigned to us every day was reasonable. Arguing with parents and teachers would be easy, but how does a 12-year-old argue with Plato?

First of all, the guy is dead. Second, he seemed to be reasonably reputable. I mean, there are statues of him in the halls of the most prestigious schools around the world, artistic renderings of his likeness in the history books, and whole rooms devoted to his writings in the libraries. Third, even if he was alive, I had a feeling he could out-argue me anytime, any-where, on any topic, not to mention on my "home-work load" theories.

Empowered by the pride I felt that I could even come close to grasping the basic thoughts of Plato and Aristotle, I went on to the rest of the ancient Greek mind-wrestling all-stars: Heraclitus, Parmenides, Epicurus, Diogenes, Zeno, Democritus...

Although at times frustrating and confusing, the sheer joy of intellectual challenge, of exercising my mental faculties in trying to comprehend their theo-ries, proved irresistible to me. Cynicism, hedonism, stoicism, sophism, pluralism, monism, materialism, fatalism, optimism, etc., all slowly became part of my vocabulary. But this progress only whetted my appetite.

I remember overhearing two undergraduate philos-ophy students talking in a café one evening about

German philosopher Hegel, his "dialectic," and its influence on Marx's social theories. As I was over 20 centuries behind them in my philosophical studies and much younger than they, I couldn't understand a thing they were talking about, but it all somehow sounded so much more complex, more intricate, even more important, than what I had encountered so far. They discussed it with such concern and fervor, as if their lives depended on the outcome, yet with an ease of someone who fully owns the subject at hand.

I wanted to have a mind like theirs. I wanted to know more: about the history of philosophy and human thought, about the evolution of philosophical theories, about the works and ideas of all major philosophers, not just ancient Greeks.

Instinctively, I was looking for something significant, definitive, eternal. I didn't realize that, by the time I would be mentally capable to thoroughly read and understand the works that indeed pointed to the Truth—the ultimate, spiritual and, therefore, indestructible Truth—the intellectual air of my society I breathed in daily would be so saturated by the deadly toxins of atheism and socialism that it would prevent me from even glancing at such Truth, much less accepting it.

Having been raised by parents who were raised by the Communist Party and taught by teachers who were taught by the Party, through curricula created by the Party, my view of religion, particularly

Christianity, as an atrophied relic of the past, was absolute and unchangeable. No treatise, thesis, novel or poem could change my mind. It remained something that only gullible, shallow and uneducated people could ever consider seriously.

Indeed, by the time I read Augustine, Aquinas, Spinoza, Kierkegaard, etc., at the age of 16, the Divine they so intensely probed and analyzed remained for me just an intriguing figment of humanity's imagination. They, and many other masters of philosophy throughout history, skillfully and competently considered the Divine, and were all definitely worth academic contemplation and discussion. Still, they were, for me, just leftovers from humanity's intellectual and cultural evolution.

Nothing anybody could say, write or argue at the time, no matter how convincing and reasonable it may have seemed, could have persuaded me otherwise. My life appeared to be proof enough that what my teachers, my parents, and my books taught me was the truth—man creates his own happiness; man shapes his own destiny; man does not need God to be happy.

Undoubtedly, this mindset brought great delight and pleasure to those atheist masterminds who plotted my generation's future. Thankfully, and unbeknownst to all but to the Creator they so arrogantly dismissed, their poisonous joy would be short lived.

XI

TWO years passed since my encounter with the American tourist, and my recollection of him became but a blur. I was now 18, getting ready to graduate with a bachelor's degree in music, and was slowly—physically and mentally—preparing for the mandatory 18 months service in the Yugoslavian army. One evening, just as I was about to leave for a rehearsal, a telephone ring broke the silence in my family's apartment. As I answered, I heard the slow, melodious drawl of the southern American-English language greeting me from the other side of the wire. My mind started racing, flooded by a frenzy of unexpectedly awakened, pleasant memories—Mr. Cameraman, Mr. Safari Hat, Mr. "Aigs and Baikun" (what? no "griyuts"?), Mr. "Uhmerikin" tourist... Mr. Kelley Travis himself.

He was calling from his hometown of Jackson, Mississippi. By the time I came to my senses, he was describing how he had recently played that concert tape of mine he took as a last-minute souvenir for someone at one of the universities in Louisiana. They were so impressed that they offered me a full scholarship to continue my studies there, if I so desired. Did

I hear that right? Did I understand that correctly? Would I like to continue my studies in the U.S.?

Everybody in eastern Europe wanted to "continue their studies" in the U.S.! In addition to being known as the land of economic opportunities, for us young musicians, the U.S. always represented the land of unlimited artistic possibilities, as well. We dreamed about it the way children dream about fairyland—so magical and extraordinary, yet so far away, so untouchable and unreachable, that it just had to remain in the realm of dreams. And yet, here it was, offered to me on a platter. How lucky was that? Where do I sign, please?

But all at once it dawned on me that in all the excitement over the news, I had forgotten about the army service hanging over me, which had to be fulfilled before I would be allowed to leave the country for any substantial period of time. I informed Mr. Travis of this fact. He said that, in that case, he would call me back when I finished my tour of duty, in 18 months, to see if I was still interested in coming to the U.S. As our telephone conversation ended, I was crushed. How was it possible that such a great opportunity came my way, and then disappeared in the blink of an eye?

Yes, I knew he said he would call me back in 18 months, and that it seemed like the whole thing was simply postponed, but do you seriously think that anybody would remember to make a certain phone call in 18 months? I surely didn't think so. It's not as if we were talking about next week, or even next month. No. We were talking about a year and a half—18 months... 84 weeks... 547 days. Nobody could remember to make a call in 547 days. Not to mention that, in my mind, the chances were even slimmer that the school Mr. Travis mentioned would keep the offer on the table for such a long period of time.

Can you image how it felt to have had America so close you could taste it, just to have it pulled away from you the moment it crossed from dream into reality? If you were born in America, probably not. But if you were born just about anywhere else in the world, you certainly know the magic that the name of this country evokes in the minds of those looking at it from the outside. Yes, some may hate its politics, foreign policies, secularism, Protestant heritage, media, even its language, but they all still want to come here. For, regardless of all their grudges and objections, they know that only here, only in America, can they have that which they can't find in their own countries—real freedom, real justice, and real economic opportunity.

I certainly knew that fact. Although I didn't feel as though my life in Yugoslavia was filled with suffering and depravity, and although I really enjoyed my friends, family, and all of my musical and academic endeavors there, America still held a promise of life and opportunities simply not feasible in my country. And all of that, having briefly appeared as an actual possibility for my own future, in my mind became just a dream once again. I simply had to accept it, and move on. After all, there was nothing I could do about it. But there was, and is, a power beyond my understanding Who indeed could do something about it: the power Whose plan was just beginning to unfold, quietly leading me to a place that makes even America look jaded.

Darko (19 years old) performing as a soldier in the Yugoslavian National Army.

XII

I C A M E back home from serving in the army with renewed appreciation and yearning for the civilian life. Being "Corporal Velichkovski" and playing war games just didn't agree with me. All the yelling and screaming, all the eager displays of power, all the blatant political brainwashing, all the mind-numbing, pointless drills, all of it made me miss the "outside world" terribly. And now, I was finally home. The nightmare was over, and I didn't have to salute the brass on anybody's shoulders anymore, practice parade steps and formations, sleep in trenches full of mud, or clean my rifle a thousand times a day. I was a civilian again, and there was no end to my joy.

A couple of weeks passed after my return, and my life in Belgrade was slowly returning to normal. Welcome-home parties were over, the excitement over the novelty of being back in Belgrade was wearing off, and it was back to cafés, concerts, rehearsals, books and recordings. And then, in the middle of one of those ordinary afternoons in my family's apartment, the telephone rang, and as I answered, I once again heard that familiar southern drawl—Mr. Kelley Travis... calling again, after a year and a half. He didn't forget.

I forgot, mind you, but he didn't. Enough to put you to shame, isn't it? He was calling to say that the scholarship offer by that university in Louisiana was still valid, and to ask if I wanted him to accept the offer on my behalf and begin my registration process and immigration paperwork. He also mentioned that if I could, I should come several weeks before school started, to get somewhat acclimated and familiar with the new culture and environment. He and his wife would be my American host family, he said, and I could stay with them in Jackson, Mississippi, during that time. Yes, Mr. Kelley... please... thank you... thank you... thank you... yes, we will talk again, soon... thank you... good-bye.

That was it. In just a few minutes my life took a totally unexpected turn. America, once again, danced in front of my eyes, like a beautiful, captivating girl everyone admired from afar... only, this time, she was asking me to dance with her. It was time for me to get ready for the ball.

As worried as they were to let me go, and as hard as it was to afford such a journey, my parents supported me in pursuing this once-in-a-lifetime opportunity. They sold our only prized possession, a Russian-made upright piano that had a prominent place in our living room for years, and took out all of their savings to buy my airline ticket to Houston, Texas, and to give me some emergency spending money. Neither my parents nor I were aware of the fact that the "emergency fund" I was given, on which you could live for a month in Yugoslavia, wasn't enough to survive even a couple of days in the U.S. But, as the saying goes, ignorance is bliss.

By the way, those of you familiar with the U.S. geography have undoubtedly noticed that my final destination, Houston, Texas, is very far away from the Travis family hometown of Jackson, Mississippi—500 miles away. Just to pick me up from the airport, those poor people would have to drive nine hours to Houston, and then, of course, nine hours back to Jackson. Why didn't I get a ticket to one of the much closer international airports, like New Orleans or Memphis? As embarrassing as it is to admit, here it is—the travel agency in Belgrade where I bought the ticket had only a tiny little map of the U.S., and on that map, Houston, Texas, was only about an inch away from Jackson, Mississippi. How far could it really be, if it's only an inch away? It was cheaper, too, than the other alternatives. Only an inch away, and yet cheaper—no contest. I'll have one of those, please.

Can you imagine the "joy" of my host family, as I called to tell them that I got my ticket to the U.S. and would need them to pick me up at so-and-so date and time, at the airport... in Houston. They were probably thinking, "Houston? Why not San Francisco,

Chicago or New York? If we are going to see American metropolises, there are nicer ones than Houston." Just kidding, of course.

The Travises not only didn't mention anything about it but, in spite of my obvious misjudgment, enthusiastically expressed their pleasure and excitement that we would meet soon. They mercifully spared my ego, and allowed my ignorance of the U.S. geography to continue parading as "consumer savvy"... at least until the day I was to spend nine hours in the back seat of their car, traveling that one inch on the map.

XIII

THE 747 was in its final approach to the airport in Houston. Through the airplane windows, I could see the endless lights of the city illuminating the evening sky like a giant Christmas tree. As I was seated in the middle of the row, looking toward the window, I couldn't help noticing the face of the woman seated in the window seat. She was anxiously looking at the city lights below and crying. Her tears were staining her army uniform, and she quickly dabbed the spots dry with a handkerchief, all the while stealing brief teary peeks through the window, as if not to miss anything. It was obvious that she was coming back home after a long absence, and her excitement was overwhelming.

I, on the other hand, was looking at those same city lights almost paralyzed by fear and concern over what's to come. What if the Travises were not there waiting for me? What if this whole thing about coming to America was just somebody's idea of a joke? Why would I even think that some American family would care about me? What if Mr. Travis was in Malaysia right now, laughing at my naïve foolishness?

After all, I really didn't know the man. We only spent a couple of hours together in Belgrade, four years earlier, hardly enough to get to know anybody. All of those things that my parents tried to talk to me about, and that I nonchalantly dismissed as typical parents' paranoia, were now becoming all too real. So real, that my eyes were beginning to tear up as my mind raced, trying to resolve all possible disastrous scenarios.

So, here we were, an American soldier and I, seated next to each other, looking through the airplane window at the bright lights of Houston, crying... in unison... for two diametrically opposite reasons. Can't you just see it as the opening scene of some new Francis Ford Coppola movie? In the TV commercial for it, over the scene of the two of us crying, and accompanied by a lush symphonic soundtrack, a scrolling text would silently exclaim the film critics' one liners –

" 'The Immigrant'—a touching story of human struggle and courage in the midst of insurmountable odds... stirring and soul-searching... a triumph! "

And just as the plane touched down, the soldier turned toward me and said: "Home? Mine, too. Isn't it beautiful? There is no place like home, is there?" I just nodded speechlessly, sparing her all the confusion my thickly accented reply would have undoubtedly brought about. She was right, though. There is no place like home... but mine was thousands of miles away.

The plane landed and taxied to the gate. Everyone

around me got up from their seats, collected their belongings, lined up for the exit, and, as usual with airplane passengers all over the world, were propping themselves up on their toes, looking over each other's shoulders to see what's taking so long. They had places to go, people to see, and couldn't wait to get out. Not me. I just sat there, waiting for the last passenger to exit, so I could come out alone to meet my destiny.

Finally, as the cabin emptied, I walked down the aisle, through the exit door and into the terminal. What I saw defied any reason, expectation, or explanation. Hundreds of people were standing around the gate in a chaotic semicircle. As I appeared at the gate they broke out in loud cheers, some waving small American flags, and some large red, white, and blue handmade signs bearing my name. Handshakes and hugs abounded from all sides, and I felt totally confused and perplexed.

Were these people positive that they were waiting for me? Where were the Travises? Would I even recognize Mr. Travis after four years? How embarrassing would it be to look him in the eye and not even recognize him? And who were all these people mobbing me and cheering as if I was some movie star, or at the very least their long lost rich relative?

Suddenly, out of this mass of people, a familiar face appeared in front of me—Mr. Travis. "Darko!" he said with a big smile on his face. "We were beginning to worry that you missed your plane. This is my wife, Jean."

Noticing my puzzled gaze across the crowd, he continued, "And those people carrying signs and flags are our friends from Houston. As for the rest, they are the passengers from your plane and the people who were waiting for their flights in the terminal when we got here. I suppose they thought that, with all the flags and signs we were carrying, we were meeting somebody famous; so they all stayed around to see who it is. As you appeared, they all joined in cheering and waving; pushing even Jean and me out of the way with their handshakes and hugs. Sorry about that. It sure is good to see you again. Let's go get your luggage."

Sorry about that? About what? He was there, Mrs. Travis was there, and their friends were there, waiting for me. That's all I needed. I wasn't dreaming the whole thing. He wasn't joking after all. He wasn't in Malaysia, drinking cocktails and laughing at me. As for the enthusiastic crowd of onlookers, it didn't hurt at all to be treated like a celebrity, even if it was by mistake.

Still dazed by the whole experience, still speechless, I smiled and followed the Travises and their friends to the baggage claim, looking at the oversized red, white, and blue sign one of them carried—"Welcome to America, Darko." Indeed.

XIV

As if that unexpected welcome wasn't enough for one day, that very same evening, as we settled around the dinner table at one of the Travis family friends' house, Mr. Travis shared with me some startling news. Apparently, while I was still in the army, the Travises traveled to New York City for a week-long tourist visit. With them they carried the concert tape I gave Mr. Travis in Belgrade, along with all the other tapes they liked to listen to on the road. After a few days in the city, Mr. Travis put my tape in his Walkman and, while listening to it, decided that someone at The Juilliard School of Music, one of the most prestigious music conservatories in the world, needed to hear it as well. Maybe they would show some interest, he figured, and besides, it couldn't hurt to get an opinion from someone at such a notable institution.

So off he went to The Juilliard School, and there tried his best to talk the guards into letting him in. He didn't count on the fact that only those with official Juilliard IDs and appointment notices were allowed in. Having neither, he was turned away. Back at his hotel, he telephoned the Juilliard administration office and asked for an appointment. The first available time they could see him was days after he and Mrs. Travis were to depart from New York. It seemed like a dead end and not worth pursuing after all. But then he decided to try something highly unusual.

While he was practicing law, Mr. Travis was a trial attorney for U.S. Department of Justice. Although retired, he still had his U.S. Department of Justice badge. He put on his suit and tie, went back to The Juilliard School, flashed his badge at the guards, and got in. Just like that.

He went up to the administration offices, asked for the list and schedules of the clarinet professors, found one that was teaching at the time, and went straight to his room. The professor whose lesson he interrupted was Mr. David Weber, one of the last true orchestral clarinet legends and one of the most respected clarinet professors in the world. Of course, Mr. Travis didn't know any of these details. He just knocked at his door, introduced himself, and started telling him about me and the concert tape he wanted him to hear.

Well, apparently, Mr. Weber wasn't amused at all by Mr. Travis' request, and didn't make any effort to hide the fact that he was upset over such a rude interruption of his lesson. If Mr. Travis wanted him to hear the tape, Mr. Weber said, closing the door, he should pursue the matter within established administrative procedures and channels. He probably thought that would be the last time he saw or heard from that peculiar southerner. He didn't know Mr. Travis.

The very next morning, Mr. Travis returned. This time he didn't interrupt the lesson, but waited in front of Mr. Weber's room with a cassette boom box in his hands, preloaded with my tape, and ready to press that "Play" button the moment Mr. Weber came out. The lunch period came, and Mr. Weber opened the door of his room and ran straight into Mr. Travis, who immediately turned on his boom box and played my tape for Mr. Weber while following him down the hallway and into the elevator.

After a few minutes of this treatment, desperate Mr. Weber agreed to sit down in the professors' lounge with Mr. Travis and listen to the tape. After fully reviewing my performance, Mr. Weber said that he would be interested in working with me, and that if I indeed played and sounded like that taped performance, I had a really good chance of getting a scholarship, as well. Of course, first I would have to officially apply for The Juilliard School, be accepted to the auditions, perform and pass the live audition, and take and pass all the other admission tests. Mr. Weber was willing to commit to guaranteeing my acceptance to the upcoming live auditions based on the tape he just heard, and asked Mr. Travis to keep him posted on my plans.

Without hesitation, Mr. Travis filled out all the

preliminary application forms in my name and picked up all the necessary paperwork and documents, just in case I wanted to pursue this opportunity any further. He decided not to share this whole Juilliard episode with me over the phone while I was still in Yugoslavia, as he was afraid of creating misunderstanding and confusion in my mind.

But now that I was finally in the States, he made sure that I fully understood the situation, urged me to think hard about the whole thing, and make a decision pretty soon. The calendar was forcing the issue—auditions in New York were scheduled for March, and my semester in Louisiana was to begin two months earlier, in January. I came to the U.S. based on my scholarship to the university in Louisiana. If I enrolled and started attending there it would be entirely inappropriate to change my mind later. So, the question really was whether I should go for the guaranteed scholarship in Louisiana or forfeit it in exchange for the possibility of a scholarship in New York.

Now, to understand my dilemma fully, you need to know that The Juilliard School was the educational institution serious young musicians like me around the world dreamed of attending. To study at Juilliard was like studying at Harvard, Yale and Oxford, all at once. Unfortunately, we saw this prospect as a largely impossible proposition. Why? The key word here is "astronomical."

First, the tuition, by most of the world standards was astronomical, as was the cost of living in New York City. Second, the number of students applying for the few open spots every year was astronomical. Third, the audition standards were astronomical. All in all, the chances of not making it through the auditions, or not being able to afford the cost, were—yes, you guessed it—astronomical.

And yet, at first glance, it seemed the doors were slightly cracked opened for me. A very exciting and surprising development, full of possibility. On the other hand, that guaranteed full scholarship in Louisiana was exactly that—a guaranteed full scholarship. How do you turn down such an offer for a possibility?

But studying at The Juilliard School in New York City wasn't just any "possibility," and its lure proved irresistible, as risky as it was. A few days after my arrival to the U.S., while still in Houston, I informed the Travises of my decision—I would forfeit the scholarship in Louisiana and officially apply for the auditions at The Juilliard School. Once again, my life took an unexpected turn, and I couldn't wait to see the end of this curve.

XV

TRAVELING nine hours that one inch on the map, from Houston to Jackson, was indeed a humbling experience. I found out that America was much, much larger than I ever imagined, and learned not to underestimate the vastness of even an inch on its map. As we arrived in Jackson, the Travises helped me settle into one of the guest rooms in their house, which was to become my temporary American home. Actually, since Mr. and Mrs. Travis' children were all grown and living on their own, I had the whole second floor to myself—my own bathroom, my own bedroom, my own practice room... How lucky, I thought, how lucky.

All of my life I lived with my father, mother and brother in a compact one-bedroom apartment the size of the Travis's garage. My parents slept on the pullout sofa in the living room, while my brother and I shared the tiny bedroom. No whining for privacy there, as you can imagine. Since we lived in an apartment building, and in such close quarters, I was restricted to practicing my clarinet at certain hours of the day. Often, after finishing my homework, I had to take a city bus back to school to practice. And now, here I was, having all this space, just for myself, where I could practice as much as I wanted all day—courtesy of the Travis' kindness.

And as if that wasn't enough, they fed me (of all things, Heinz ketchup and Hershey's chocolate quickly seduced my taste buds), clothed me (blue jean overalls were my newfound favorite American garment), and helped me get a driver's license. (Driving Mr. Travis's Lincoln Towncar, which was the size of my Belgrade apartment building, on Interstate 55 in Jackson, which looked as wide as a 747 runway to me, was an indescribable thrill.) They also paid my Juilliard application fees (being The Juilliard School, these fees were no small change), got me a library card (I really missed my books, and had planned to reread as many as possible in English), and introduced me to all of their family and friends (we are talking an army of people here, folks: from lawyers and doctors, to teachers, judges, and housewives, from infants to 90-year-olds). They truly made me feel as one of their own, and did their best to help me adapt to my new environment.

And believe me, I needed all the help I could get. Everything around me was so new and different... overwhelmingly different. First of all, everywhere I turned, there were choices, choices, and some more choices. You want cereal? Aisle 3. Six miles of cereals—in 30,000 different flavors. Deodorant? Aisle 16. Three acres of deodorants—sprays, roll-ons, sticks, in 15,000 distinct scents. Jeans? Second floor. 960 racks of jeans—originals, stone-washed, riveted, bleached, boot-cut, relaxed-fit, overalls, baggies, low-riders, bermudas, wide-bottoms, torn knees, non-riveted, three-quarter length, stitched seats, in 20,000 different brands.

Even the carwashes had menus here. I couldn't believe it. How many ways can you wash a car, anyway? Well, do you want your car washed? Around the corner. Regular, soaking, with brushes, brushless, early bird special, premium, air-dried, hand-dried, full-tank finest, waxed, the works. And we are not done yet. Do you need a car fragrance with it? We can give your car that distinct scent of lemon, pine, orange, fresh breeze, chocolate, lime, coconut, baby powder... even that elusive new car smell. The new car smell? You can buy that? I could die now, for I have finally seen it all.

Do you see what I mean by being overwhelmed by choices? Where I came from, no one spent any mental energy on choices, for there were none. As an example, we had one kind of cereal, but since we used it as food for hamsters and parakeets (for no self-respecting Yugoslavian would eat something that looks like bird food) we didn't really see any need for choices there.

Hot dogs, bacon, ham, and eggs were our breakfast preferences. But it didn't seem as if there were any need for overwhelming choices there, either. The breakfast food we had available in the grocery store was: one kind of hot dog—brown, oblong, in murky liquid, six inches long; two kinds of bacon—one with a lot of fat and the other with even more fat; two kinds of ham—sliced and not sliced; and two kinds of eggs—broken and not broken. That's it.

See how much easier and quicker our grocery shopping was? There was one kind of deodorant—white spray can with the word "Deodorant" printed on it, one kind of jeans—blue, made in China, Levi's copy, and certainly one kind of car wash—bucket and rag, self-service hand-dry, of course. Very straight, very simple, very socialist.

But, oh how little it takes to turn even the most dedicated socialist into an enthusiastic, free-market-loving, Wall-Street-hugging defender of capitalism. Just give him some real freedom of choice, add a bar of Hershey's milk chocolate with almonds, a pair of Levi's stonewashed overalls, a bowl of Kellogg's granola cereal with raisins and walnuts, a dab of Gillette's clear musk deodorant, and that new car scent after a brushless carwash. Stir gently, and wait to cool. Your new capitalist advocate will be ready within days. Just ask me. I know all about it.

XVI

THE Travises became my American family. They were consistently kind and caring towards me and were always there when I needed them. As days turned into weeks, I was beginning to wonder why would they want to help me. What exactly did I do to earn their kindness? How did I deserve their care? Was this a "payback" for those few days of hospitality back in Belgrade? It couldn't be. What I did for Mr. Travis, those several hours spent as his tour guide four years prior, certainly paled in comparison.

But, at least, in the case of Mr. Travis, there was a trace of a reason, as illusory as it was. As for Mrs. Travis (or Mrs. Jean, as I called her), I had not even met her prior to my arrival in the U.S., much less had a chance to do her any favors for which she would feel obligated to reciprocate. Yet she gladly and graciously took on the role of my "American mother," with all the implications and connotations of that term, and that was truly puzzling (and humbling) to me.

But there was also something else different about her, and, at first, I didn't connect the two. While Mr. Travis generally kept his spiritual beliefs private, Mrs. Jean was very open about her Christian faith. She prayed before every meal, had her "quiet time" every

Kelley Travis (far right) with Darko's parents and brother.

morning, used phrases "Thank God," "In God's own time," and "God willing," like she really meant them, attended Bible studies, Sunday school, and worship services, and had her well-worn Bibles and biblical literature lying all over the house, reading them every chance she could. Of all these, her devoted reading of the Bible served as a clear clue to me as to the nature of her belief; not why she believed, but what she believed, which made the reason for her belief even more puzzling to me.

As surprising as it may be, I had read the Bible many times growing up. Not as the precept of spiritual truths in Bible studies or Sunday schools, of course; but for my philosophy, history and cultural anthropology classes, together with the works of Buddhism, Hinduism, Islam, Confucianism, and the other world religious writings.

As I mentioned earlier, in order to diminish the importance of the biblical writings, the communist curriculum bundled its study together with all the religions of the world, in effect making them all equal, as nothing more than figments of humanity's wishful spiritual imagination. Furthermore, to truly cement this notion of the nature of Christianity in our minds, our ever-so-thorough communist master-minds created student dictionaries to be used extensively in our studies, and which contained the following definition of the Bible: "The Bible is a collection of fantastic stories, fairy tales, with no scientific or historical bases, used by corrupt western political powers to prey upon unsuspecting nations."

Is there any wonder that the belief in anything "otherworldly," and especially Christianity, was unequivocally and unquestionably beyond the realm of possibility for me? And is there any wonder that I was completely astounded by Mrs. Jean's just-as-unquestionable adherence to that same Christian belief? If her kindness was simply puzzling, then these blatant, unapologetic displays of her religiosity were wildly perplexing to me. I mean, she seemed to be an intelligent, educated and reasonable woman, and yet she held strongly to those antiquated and sim-pleminded Christian ideas that I thought most of modern civilization had long left behind.

Now, I knew that Americans believed and lived in a different social and economic system than the one I left behind, but I was not prepared to meet their spiritual heritage up close and personal. I just assumed

Darko (21 years old) in Jackson, Mississippi, with Dr. and Mrs. Schuyler Batson and Mrs. Jean Travis (far right).

that, like ours, it was mostly extinct and forgotten. But here it was, personified in this kind, caring, but also sensible and rational woman. This phenomenon simply defied explanation in my mind, and I just had to accept it and learn to live with it. That's all there was to it.

Mrs. Jean believed what she believed, for whatever mysterious reasons, and that belief seemed to define and guide her completely. Slowly, it became apparent to me that her attitude toward me, her kindness and care, stemmed from the same inexplicable source. And while I wished she would somehow discover the truth and recognize the intellectual naiveté of her faith, I couldn't actually find any faults with the effects that faith had apparently produced in her character.

All of my life I was taught to think of religious people as foolish and naïve, as flawed and weak characters and minds, as atheists' intellectual inferiors. I suppose it was easy to hold and defend such an opinion in the environment where I had never known any actual, practicing Christians. But how could I possibly reconcile such convictions with what I saw in Mrs. Jean?

I couldn't, and that dilemma baffled me immensely. But I simply concluded that she must have been a rare exception, and that, by and large, what I was taught about Christians still held true. At the time, I simply wasn't aware of the fact that virtually all of the people I met in those first few weeks in this country were also Christians and that my presumptions would soon be challenged again, even more distressingly.

XVII

ONE Sunday morning, three weeks after my arrival, the Travises asked me if I would join them for the worship service at their church—First Baptist Church in downtown Jackson. After all they had done for me, how could I refuse? So I put on my white shirt and a tie, my black "concert" pants and shiny shoes, and off we went... to church... for a worship service. I couldn't believe it—me, at a Christian worship service. And I thought carwash menus were the height of the improbable.

Naturally, I expected to find a small group of disillusioned and irrational people there, and I honestly dreaded the encounter. What would I do and say in their presence? What exactly is the proper "worship service etiquette"? Actually, forget the etiquette, what do you do at a Christian service at all? Having never attended one, I was considerably anxious.

The churches where I came from were mostly museums, where one would go to admire historical pieces of art, frescoes and mosaics, not places of worship. Every once in a while you would see some old ladies and men go in on Sunday mornings, or hear strange singing sounds resonate through the windows, or maybe even catch a glimpse, through the cracked-opened-doors, of some old farmer kneeling at the altar, but none of these recollections was very helpful in my present predicament. I was about to enter into what I imagined to be the dark, mysterious, and above all, delusional world of Christian worship, and I had no idea what to do or how to act.

Needless to say, I was seriously beginning to regret accepting the Travises' invitation, but there was no going back now. We were already getting into the parking lot, and my last few desperate hopes for a flat tire, a blizzard, or even a biblical plague of locusts, were cruelly shattered as Mrs. Jean proclaimed with a smile: "Well, here we are." See, I knew there was no God.

The first surprise I encountered that day was the grandiose size and the "unaged" look of the church building we were about to enter. There it was, the size of a city block, impeccably built, with traces of neo-Gothic lines, rising high over surrounding structures. Not ancient, not even old, but relatively new, with not even a hint of deterioration on its vast exposed surfaces.

The newness is what really struck me as very unusual. Who, in this day and age still builds churches, I wondered, and why? Touring Europe, as well as my own country, I had seen thousands of churches. I had even visited the famous ones—the Notre Dame cathedral, the Duomos in Milan and Florence, the Cathedral of Saint Mark in Venice, the Vatican's

Saint Peter's, Istanbul's Hagia Sofia, as well as count-less lesser-known Eastern Orthodox and Catholic churches, but they were all built long ago, some many centuries ago.

Their age, despite their timeless aesthetic beauty, signified to me the outdated, irrelevant beliefs their architecture and art represented. I was taught that as humanity progressed through the intellectual evolu-tion, as we slowly chiseled away the shackles of igno-rance and blind faith, we had less need for "other-worldly" doctrines and, therefore less need to build those architectural relics of regress and backwardness. In my mind, that assumption meant that the building of churches ceased long ago in all but perhaps a few third world countries. And yet, there it was, right in front of me, imposing and undeniable.

As we slowly proceeded toward its striking, over-sized front doors, another "phenomenon" caught my eye—the sheer number of people heading toward it from all sides. Surely all these people are not going into this church, I thought. But they were. And as we finally entered the sanctuary, their number swelled not to hundreds, but thousands. Thousands! Regular people—young, old, families... bright-eyed, civil and polite, not the half-crazed, anti-social, intellectually deprived fanatics of my social studies textbooks.

Walking down the aisle, the Travises paused every few steps greeting others, being greeted, and introduc-ing me as their guest. Mrs. Jean would lean over toward me and say a few words after every introduction, telling me a bit about the people I was meeting—teachers, businessmen, nurses, judges, secretaries, doctors, lawyers... And then, we finally reached our pew and sat down. And just in time, for I really needed to sit down and clear my head from this most surprising experience.

I was speechless, overwhelmed by the whole scene unfolding around me—thousands of ordinary people, singing, praying, worshiping, as one. Not a trace of shame or embarrassment, of awkwardness or shyness. Joy in their eyes, joy in their voices... joy, not wariness. Was I awake, I wondered? For, this experience was beyond *Alice In Wonderland,* beyond *The Wizard Of Oz,* beyond the limits of my wildest imagination.

As the service progressed, my mind raced faster and faster. My teachers, my books, my parents... were they all wrong? Not about religion, for I knew they were certainly right about that, but about these people, religious people, Christians. These people were definitely not social misfits with weak minds, out of touch with reality. There was a full spectrum of society there—homemakers, professionals, academics, parents, single adults, grandparents, students... people just like the ones I left behind in my country. And yet, they were all there, in that sanctuary, unapologetically praying and worshiping. How incredible, I thought. How incredible.

It became painfully obvious to me that my concept

of Christians would have to undergo a major adjustment, to say the least. But that conclusion came with some frightening possible consequences. If I was to grant Christians the same mind, intellect, and social intelligence that I granted those I left behind, then Christian ideas could not be dismissed *a priori* as spiritual relics, lacking depth and credibility, either.

But that was impossible. How could anyone seriously consider fairy tales? Can anyone with a trace of intelligence and education really do that? It seemed like an impossible proposition, yet perfectly fair, logical, and in line with my startling discovery about Christians. A paradox, I thought, I discovered a paradox. That's the only way I could look at it. Zeno's paradoxes were child's play in comparison. This one was enough to blow your atheist mind to a million pieces—intelligent, civilized, educated... Christians. Reconcile that, Darko.

Luckily, the service ended just in time to spare my desperate mind from yet another round of hopeless and painful wondering. As we exited the sanctuary, Mrs. Jean turned to me and said, "I know you must be concerned, maybe even a little frightened, over what the future might hold for you and over all the obstacles that might come your way. But I want you to know that I am praying for you, and my Sunday school, they are praying for you, and my whole church, they are praying for you. Don't worry. We are praying for you."

XVIII

E VER since I had arrived in the U.S., I read everything I could get my hands on, with the help of my trusty dictionary, to build my English language skills and vocabulary. I tried to memorize as many new words as I possibly could on a daily basis. One evening, four weeks after my arrival, having just finished practicing my clarinet for the day, I decided to find and memorize a few more new English words and phrases.

As I didn't want to disturb the Travises by roaming through their living room for reading material so late in the evening, I pulled out my U.S. immigration papers and began going over the text searching for unfamiliar terms and looking up their definitions. What caught my eye, for some reason, were the handwritten scribbles next to the words printed in somewhat faded red ink in my passport on the page with all the U.S. visa seals. By the time I finished deciphering their collective meaning, the leisurely evening I was enjoying turned into a living nightmare.

The text I read spelled not merely ordinary words, but words that had the power to turn my life upsidedown. In essence, it said that I had 30 days from the time of my entry into the U.S. to report and enroll at the educational institution that guaranteed my immigration visa (that university in Louisiana which I never even saw, much less enrolled at, remember?). The failure to do so within the aforementioned period of time, the text carried on, would render my immigration status delinquent and, therefore, me an illegal alien. An illegal alien? As in hunted, jailed and thrown out of the country with no chance of returning legally... ever? I had 30 days to do what? How is it that I missed this "minute detail" of my visa conditions?

Perhaps that's what the immigration officer at the airport in Houston was saying as he was checking my documents and scribbling in my passport. But I wasn't sure, since I hadn't understood a word he said. I did remember nodding at him as he spoke, with my eyes squinting, straining to project that look of comprehension, but all the while thinking how desperately I needed to improve my English, because his words made absolutely no sense to me. How was I to know that my innocent pretense, in trying to avoid the embarrassment of the moment, would one day cost me so much?

Maybe it still wasn't too late to comply, I thought, desperately grasping for straws. Frantically, I turned the pages in my calendar and nervously counted the days since my arrival: 27, 28, 29... 29. It was day 29. (Actually, since this was the evening of day 29, it was day "29 and three-quarters.") The situation looked grim. In gut-wrenching panic, I ran downstairs, woke the Travises up, and in my excitement mustered only three thick accented English words, which I kept repeating for good measure, trying to convey my overwhelming concern over this alarming predicament—DAY TWENTY-NINE, DAY TWENTY-NINE!

You can just imagine my host family's horror as they saw their little immigrant guest running through their house in his pajamas, waving his passport, and yelling something that vaguely sounded like English, over and over again. I am sure their first instinct was probably to call 911, as I appeared to be in need of heavy medication. Instead, they sat me on their sofa, told me to slow down, breathe, and try to explain what the hysteria was all about.

After a brief inquiry into the matter, the Travises realized the gravity of my situation. If something wasn't done within a little over 24 hours, America would once again, and this time permanently and hopelessly, become just a distant, untouchable dream for me. Within minutes, they decided we should drive to New Orleans at once, the location of the nearest immigration office at the time. We would spend the night at a hotel, wake up early the next morning, and line up in one of those humongous lines that form daily in front of the immigration building, hoping for some understanding and compassion from the officials.

The trip took about three hours, and we arrived at our hotel in New Orleans well after midnight, predictably exhausted. Going through the motions of check-in at the front desk, we noticed unusual activity in the lobby behind us. The steady stream of people carrying musical instrument cases into the hotel and disappearing up the elevator was hard to miss.

Noticing our curiosity about this unusual scene, the front desk clerk offered an explanation. It was the night of the annual jam session of the New Orleans Jazz Club. Apparently, once a year this large group of local jazz enthusiasts and musicians pick a different venue for a night of collective musical "jamming." This year's venue was to be the restaurant on the top floor of our hotel, where the Jazz Club fully intended to "jam," while we, the hotel guests, were sleeping. I am not sure how those two activities were going to work simultaneously, but that was the unfolding situation anyway.

Since I never went anywhere without my clarinet in tow, this trip was no exception. What is amazing to me now, looking back on it, is that this young fool was hoping to get a few minutes of practicing even on that ultimate "day 30." Hello! Anybody home? I was about to be jailed, deported back to Yugoslavia, and forbidden ever to come back to the States, and I still thought that practicing a few minutes here and there throughout the day was a sensible idea.

On the other hand, Mr. Travis was a bit more realistic about the whole situation. Knowing that I had my clarinet with me, he suggested that I might want to join the Jazz Club's jam session if I wasn't too tired, and play a bit with some of the local jazz groups, since "this might be the last chance you get," as he put it.

Just for the record, let me share something with you. If you ever offer to host a foreign exchange student, or any recent immigrants, please don't use the phrase "This might be the last chance you get." It sounds incredibly ominous to us, more than you might imagine, and it makes it impossible to sleep. But since my host family was not aware of this psychological reality, and since the phrase couldn't be retracted and now sleeping indeed ceased to be an option, I took the elevator up to the top floor and played through the night with great jazz and blues musicians from New Orleans.

The morning came in what seemed like the blink of an eye. It was time to say goodbye to my new musical friends from the Jazz Club, go downstairs and wake the Travises, and then really "face the music"—at the Immigration and Naturalization Service office, of course. What that day would bring was anybody's guess, but none of us was really optimistic as to the outcome. It certainly appeared that my journey toward the American dream was coming to an end at its very onset and, barring a miracle, there was very little we could do about it.

Nevertheless, we were determined to go through the motions of this last resort and plead my case with the immigration officials. If nothing else, it would give me the peace of mind that I tried everything in my power to prevent the seemingly unavoidable catastrophe hanging over my head.

What I didn't know was that the power infinitely greater than mine was already at work, and that before the day was over I would be standing face to face with its omnipotence and strength. Yet another tremor of the spiritual earthquake was about to shake my ground, slowly but steadily, weakening even further the pillars of my atheist mind. Oblivious to it all, I took my place in a line at the immigration office in New Orleans, thinking, Here goes nothing! But nothing was further from the truth.

XIX

TIME and space appear to assume entirely different qualities and somehow to transcend their familiar attributes at government-run entities. Have you ever noticed how an hour at the post office seems like two? Or how a 50-yard-long line at the Department of Motor Vehicles seems 50 miles long? Or how the government seems to move at the speed of light when you owe taxes, but at the speed of a glacier when you are owed a refund?

Well, the immigration service is no exception to this natural wonder. I waited in what seemed like 74 different lines, yet there were only a few I could see in the building. I filled out what seemed like 54 different forms, yet I had only three in my hand. I spent what seemed like 92 hours waiting for my number to be called, yet the small hand on my watch moved only a few spaces. Amazing and fascinating—a modern marvel.

After filling out all the forms, waiting in numerous lines, and pleading my case several times, I found myself in the hallway of the immigration building late in the afternoon. I was being consoled by one of the immigration service representatives as he handed me back all of my documents and told me that there was nothing he could do for me. However, it wasn't all that bad, he murmured, patting me on my back, for I had almost eight hours of my legal status left, which was more than enough time to reach the Mexican border and exit the U.S. without being arrested... and yes, how fortunate I was that he doesn't have to detain me on the spot. He further explained how this miscalculation would probably remove all future chances of returning to the U.S., for I would never get another visa, after what I had done. You can see how his considerate counsel and encouragement made me feel so much better about the whole thing.

As he turned around and, softly whistling some pop tune, disappeared around the corner, I remained standing there, staring into space, lost, defeated, and utterly terrified. I could hear Mr. Travis still vigorously arguing at one of the counters, but by now I knew it was all for nothing. The ground was opening, swallowing my dreams one by one, right in the middle of that hallway, and I was completely helpless to do anything about it. Like the victim of some horrible crime, frozen by fear, watching the assailant run rampant, I stood paralyzed and stunned.

I know that to you it may not seem like such a tragedy, but to this 20-year-old it was the end of the world. First, my parents spent all of their money to send me to America. And when I say "all of their money," I mean they each made about $30 a month, and yet they purchased a $1,500 plane ticket to Houston, Texas for me. They sacrificed all of their savings, all of their salaries and even the Russian-made upright piano from our living room for that ticket. Second, I squandered the offer of a full scholarship to the university in Louisiana by deciding to apply for The Juilliard School instead. And third, I never even got a chance to go to New York for the auditions at The Juilliard School, much less to attend it, which was my life's dream. So you see, it was indeed the end of the world for me.

At the same time, I felt deep within me that I somehow deserved this sort of a tragic ending. For ever since the day I received that first phone call from Mr. Travis telling me about the scholarship in Louisiana, as much as I avoided admitting it, I truly felt the presence of some great unknown force in my life that kept opening doors for me, one after the other. There were just too many "somehows" in this story, and I had absolutely no control over any of them. That lack of control was what bothered me the most, because it rendered my own powers irrelevant. I was used to taking control of the situation, planning, working hard, executing the plan, reaching the goals on my own—practicing six hours a day and sounding good, studying eight hours a day and skipping a grade... "Somehow" wasn't acceptable in my world. "Somehow" was for the weak, shallow and gullible.

"Man creates his own happiness, he shapes his own

destiny," remember? He doesn't need any "great unknown forces" to do anything for him. He is the master of his own fate. And yet there I was, thousands of miles away from my home, from one open door to another, from one somehow to another... and then, of course, a disaster. How could I have been so naïve as to even entertain the notion that something larger than myself was possibly behind all the "somehows"?

I felt that my near-falling for that great hoax alone warranted my forced return to Yugoslavia, if for no other reason than for me to earn my stripes again. I never felt so foolish, so defeated and crushed, in my life. America was quickly and steadily fading from the horizon of my future, and the best I could do was hopelessly lament my inability to have deserved its blessings. How melodramatically arrogant, and how conspicuously atheist of me.

XX

STANDING there in the hallway of the immigration office, perplexed by such a quick demise, and still desperately trying to intellectualize the situation internally, I slowly folded the immigration papers in my hand and handed them back to Mr. Travis. I closed my eyes for a moment, gathering courage for what was inevitably to come—the mad rush to the airport and the Mexican border, hasty goodbyes, sad faces, my shocked parents and friends, and what I dreaded the most—all the regrets, all the "should-haves," "would-haves," and "might-have-beens." I opened my eyes, ready to take a step toward the exit, when I noticed that Mr. Travis was not standing next to me anymore. A man crossing my path suddenly stopped right in front of me, and studying my face, exclaimed with a big smile, "Hey, you are my clarinet player, aren't you?"

What was he talking about, I wondered. I had no idea who he was.

"I played a banjo in one of the bands you played with last night, remember? *St. Louis Blues, It Don't Mean A Thing, Ain't Misbehavin', When The Saints...* remember? And all those unusual tunes you played... man, that was something!" he continued, shaking his head.

Now, as I recollected, it seemed as though there had been 500 banjo players there that night, and how exactly I was supposed to remember this particular one was beyond me. But my puzzled look didn't slow his enthusiasm one bit. "Do you have a minute for a cup of coffee? I would like to talk to you about those strange Mediterranean rhythms you played for us last night."

A cup of coffee? In the midst of all this? I turned around scanning the crowd behind me for Mr. Travis, and saw him taking his place in yet another line, obviously intent to keep at it, regardless of the absolute hopelessness of the situation. Well, we did agree earlier in the day that we would meet in front of the building after the closing, if we got separated, so I guess I could have a cup of coffee... before I kill myself here! At this point I knew it was all over anyway. No reason to prolong the agony. I turned toward the banjo player, nodded my head in approval of his offer, and uttered: "Coffee? Coffee would be good."

I followed him through the crowd, and then down the hallway, all the while trying to remember the way so I could retrace it later, fully expecting to end up either in a cafeteria or at one those corners with a coffee machine, two half-empty coffeepots, and non-dairy creamer powder spilled all over the aluminum counter.

Instead, he led me down the hallway and through

the door of the executive suite at the end of the corridor. As we entered his office, he sat behind the most important-looking desk I had ever seen, instantly becoming the most important person I had ever met in my life. He placed his forefinger on the intercom button on his desk, looked at me, and, lifting his eyebrows, asked, "Sugar and cream?" I just nodded, pinching myself, making sure this was not simply a dream from which I could awaken at any moment to face the cruel and hard reality again. It wasn't. It wasn't a dream. That banjo player by night was indeed one of the highest Immigration Service officials by day!

And he had asked me if I had a minute to have a coffee with him? Not just a minute, Mister, and not just for coffee. I will sit here for days if you want me to... I will wash your car, cook your meals, even clean the bottom of your parakeet's cage, just help me, I thought. Do I have to tell you how in the blink of an eye my poor English ceased to be an obstacle to my social interaction, meaningful and engaging conversation, and making friends? And do I have to tell you how my new friend instantly became the best banjo player I had ever heard in my life; how miraculously I came to remember all the nuances of all the ingenious, unforgettable solos he played, and how I shamelessly told him so? I suppose not.

It seemed like an eternity before we ended our discussion on the finer points of the Balkan music I had played, and he finally thought of asking me why I was in his building. But when he did, within minutes my visa was extended and my passport stamped with all the official seals that would allow me to legally remain in the U.S.! With all the powers at his disposal, he made it all look completely natural and simple.

But by then I had a distinct feeling that this whole experience was far from "natural." Supernatural, otherworldly, spiritual, paranormal, mystical, magical, unearthly... anything but "natural." The "somehows" piled up so high that their sheer weight was crushing me. They filled my mind to overflowing and simply couldn't be ignored any longer. That great unknown force moved in my life again with such a power that I felt nothing but the most surprising and perplexing mixture of awe and gratitude.

As I attempted to convey my thankfulness to that undeniably powerful, yet kind and considerate gentleman sitting in front of me, I realized that he, in truth, didn't have anything to do with the whole thing. It's not as if he woke up that morning thinking, I have to make sure to be in that hallway at four o'clock to help Darko, right? And, although he indeed received all the profuse thanks I could muster—the thanks due him according to all the social norms—the real thanks, the true gratitude, was so clearly due elsewhere.

But where? To whom, to what? Was I to burn a goat like the Hebrews of the Old Testament? Give a twirl to a prayer wheel like Tibetan monks? Grow a beard and light incense like Orthodox priests? Shave my head like Hare Krishnas, handle crystals like Hollywood mega-stars, sing to Shiva like Hindus, put ashes on my forehead like the Pope? Start banging on drums and dance, like Indians, or eat sacred pudding, like Sikhs? What? What was I supposed to do with this overwhelming sense of gratitude? Thank my "lucky stars"? At which point exactly does luck lose its seemingly all-encompassing power of explanation, and cease to be "luck"? How many times, exactly, is one to encounter unlikely mercy and unexpected guidance before he should start considering something more profound than Carl Sagan's inanimate cosmos to thank?

I indeed needed to know at least the name of that great unknown force which so undeniably, insistently and determinedly guided my path to America and carried me to this point. But all of my life I had been told that there was nothing above and nothing below, nothing greater than man, nothing more powerful or more profound than what I could see or touch. And now I found myself at the crossroads that all atheists will experience one time or another—that dark, cold, lonely place, where there is no one to thank. My heart was full of gratefulness and awe, my mind humbled by the otherworldly touch, yet painfully entangled in the darkness of the lifeless, aimless, indifferent universe of my upbringing.

And then, out of nowhere, my whole being came

to be filled with just one thought—Mrs. Jean, back in that church in Jackson, telling me not to worry, that I was in her prayers, and that now her Sunday school and her whole church were praying for me as well. Why these thoughts? And why now? Wasn't this already confusing enough without bringing Christian prayers into it? How is it that at such a perplexing time I came to be filled with thoughts that I didn't even fully understand?

Although I intellectually understood the concept of prayer, its deeper and more profound spiritual aspects and powers were completely unknown to me. And yet, I was fully consumed and mesmerized by this uninvited reflection; for there was something irresistibly appealing, intriguing, and loving about it. I wished Mrs. Jean was there right then, so I could talk to her... about those prayers, about her joy, her confidence, her faith, her hope, her devotion... about her God.

If she knew anything or anybody well, she knew her God; she knew about the powers unseen. I wanted to have that knowledge, too... no, I needed to have it, for the fire of my intellectual, emotional and spiritual anxiety was burning so hot that no other kind of knowledge could extinguish its flames. The irresistible force of the Creator was pulling me toward Him, and now, there was no turning back.

XXI

B<small>Y</small> the time we arrived back to Jackson, it was already close to midnight. All the celebration and excitement over the miraculous turn of events in New Orleans, as well as the long drive back, exhausted our energies and took their toll. We were tired and sleepy, and ready to call it a night. I went to my room, sat on the edge of the bed, and stared at the wall, waiting for the silence to envelop me and tame the whirlwind of my mind.

And just as the silence became thick and heavy, tears came down my cheeks. Not tears of joy, or sadness; not tears of pain, or pleasure; but the tears of spiritual depravity and hunger. With each new salty drop falling from my face, the yearning grew deeper and wider, dissolving the stone in my chest, until finally my lips moved. "God," I uttered, "I really need to talk to Mrs. Jean about God." I didn't know how, but I knew that I desperately needed to find Him.

My hardened heart was breaking, crying out, just like the Bible says it would. Yes, even the stones will cry out His name, it says. In Luke 19:38-40, as Jesus was riding toward Jerusalem, on the road down the Mount of Olives, the crowd gathered and began to joyfully praise Him and glorify God. The Pharisees present at the scene demanded that Jesus rebuke the worshippers. Jesus replied, "If they keep quiet, the very stones will cry out." And, indeed, here in that winter of 1984, was a stone carved out of the rock of human pride and arrogance, for 20 years diligently shaped, hardened, and guarded by the champions of human wisdom, yet crying out the name of the eternal, ultimate Master and Lord.

The following morning, over breakfast, I shared with Mrs. Jean all about the fire of spiritual anxiety and confusion burning inside me, about the perplexing and overwhelming awe and gratitude I felt, and about the distinct sense of the presence of that great unknown force in my life which so deliberately and mercifully kept showing up at the most unlikely times and places.

While I was talking, her eyes swelled with tears. She closed them for a moment, letting a few drops slide down her cheeks, and then stood up, smiled, and picked up the Bible lying on the kitchen counter. "Here," she said, "here are all the answers you will ever need, Darko. Read it with an open heart and humble mind, and that great unknown force will make itself known to you. It is the power, the mercy, and the grace of God you seek to know about, and it is all in here, in His Word. He loves you, Darko. He loves you so much that He not only mercifully directed your path all the way to this place, but, more importantly, gave His only son for you. Jesus died on the cross so that you may live, truly live... eternally. Here. Read it and live."

She handed me the Bible, and before I had a chance to thank her, she pulled a handmade bookmark out of her pocket. "I made this bookmark a few days after your arrival, praying that one day you will use it as you read the Word of God," she said. "I've written some chapter and verse numbers on it. You might want to read those first." She placed the bookmark on the Bible I was holding and, clearing up the kitchen table, said, "Go on... I'll clean this up. You go read."

As I made my way upstairs, I couldn't help wondering about what she said, and if it could possibly be that simple. I guess in my ignorance and naïveté I expected her to share not only what I already knew about her faith, but also some other deeply mysterious and secret spiritual insights that somehow eluded me. But she didn't. She gave me the Bible.

How exactly was reading the Bible going to satisfy my longing, anyway? After all, I had read it a number of times before, alongside numerous other spiritual and religious writings originating from different cultures around the world for my cultural anthropology, history, and philosophy classes and seminars. I knew the stories, the characters, the major premises. I had to, if I wanted to make good grades on my tests.

By the time I reached my room, a flood of information safely stored in neatly compartmentalized confines of my mind came rushing out—mental leftovers of the hours, days and weeks spent preparing for exams, poring over the books on world religions:

Buddhism: Siddhartha Gautama. Born 563 BC. Modern-day Nepal. 535 BC, attains enlightenment. Assumes the title Buddha. Died 483 BC. The four noble truths. The five precepts. The eightfold path. Reincarnation. Nirvana.

Hinduism, also known as Sanatana Dharma and Vaidika Dharma: The Vedas, the Upanishads, the Mahabharata. Brahman trinity—Brahma, Vishnu, Shiva. Samsara—transmigrations of souls. Karma. The doctrine of the fourfold end of life.

Islam: Muhammad the Prophet. Born 570 AD. Died 632 AD. Allah. Mecca. Angel Jibreel. Qur'an. Hadiths. Five Pillars of faith—shahadah, salat, zakat, Ramadan fast, hajj.

Judaism: Yahweh. Creation. The fall. Israelites—God's chosen people. Abraham, Isaac, Jacob. Sacred covenant. Egyptian captivity. Moses. The law. Desert journey. Joshua. Promised land. Samuel. Saul. David. Solomon. The Temple. Israel. Judah. Torah. Talmud.

Sikhism: Shri Guru Nanek Dev Ji. Born 1469. Died 1538. Punjab, modern-day Pakistan. Gurus Nanak and Panth. Temple at Katarpur. Ten gurus.

Holy texts of Shri Guru Granth. Samsara. Karma. Reht Maryada—code of conduct, 27 articles.

Confucianism: K'ung Fu Tzu—Confucius. Born 551 BC. State of Lu, modern-day Shantung province in China. Chou dynasty. Six ethical teachings. Sacred books of Si Shu.

Taoism: Tao—the way. Lao Tse. Contemporary of Confucius. Leading texts—Tao-te-Ching and Chuang-tzu. Yin and Yang—the opposites. Ch'i—intrinsic energy. Tai Chi—meditative, healing physical movement.

And then the "Christianity compartment" came loose:

Christianity: Yahweh, God of the Hebrew Scriptures. Sacred texts—Old Testament, New Testament. Continuation of the Hebrew faith. Immaculate conception. Virgin Mary. Jesus, the Son of God, the Christ, the Messiah. John the Baptist. Disciples. Miracles. Pharisees. Romans. Pontius Pilate. Crucifixion. Resurrection. Salvation. Atonement.

Will the true God please stand up? Or at least raise your hand. Please. I really need to talk to you. Data, data and more data, that's all it was to me. Except for Christianity, perhaps. For by now, Christianity's data was beginning to assume the shape and the character of the people I was surrounded by—breathing, thinking, talking, walking, flesh and blood, like Mrs. Jean and her friends and family. It wasn't just data to be memorized for a test any longer, but much more than that—it was observable in individuals, their personal faith, and their transformed lives.

I thumbed the New Testament portion of the Bible in my hands—Matthew, Mark, Luke, John... It felt a little strange seeing those names in their English translation, especially without the preface "Saint" before them. It created the sense of a somewhat odd and unfamiliar commonness about them—"Hey, Matthew, did you see the game last night? Good to see you, John. How is the family? Luke, you gonna eat that?" Ordinary people, like you and me, not elusive and mysterious saints I always imagined them to be. What a strange mental picture, I thought—the saints of the Bible as ordinary people.

As I reflected further on what I knew about them, I realized that they were exactly that. It's just that reading the biblical texts in either their original dead languages or their translations into ancient versions of modern ones created a strong sense in me of not only an immense historical and cultural distance, but also an insurmountable personal remoteness and antiquity of characters and authors.

This time, as I read a few lines, I was immediately struck by the simple and modern use of the language, quite easily accessible even to me, regardless of my limited command of English. I turned to the first printed page, to see what kind of Bible it was, and it read: "The Living Bible." The Living Bible? What did that mean? Another strange mental picture appeared—the living words. Certainly a surprising contemplation, but one much closer to the truth of the matter than I ever suspected.

XXII

T H E words and numbers written on the bookmark were all neatly lined up along the edges,
making for an unusual border design:

Romans 3:10 / Romans 3:23-26, 5:8, 6:23 / John
3:16, Ephesians 2:1-6 / Romans 10:9-10, 10:13 / John
14:6

I opened up the Bible Mrs. Jean gave me and turned
its thin, almost transparent pages back and forth until
the book of Romans appeared under my fingers. I
found the text referenced on the bookmark already
underlined for me. Mrs. Jean sure didn't take any
chances, I thought. Chapter 3, Verse 10. Okay, God,
speak to me.

"No one is good—no one in all the world is innocent."

And then the footnote—"See Psalm 14:1-3." I
turned to Psalm 14, and its first three verses read:

"That man is a fool who says to himself, 'There is
no God'! Anyone who talks like that is warped and

evil and cannot really be a good person at all. The Lord looks down from heaven on all mankind to see if there are any who are wise, who want to please God. But no, all have strayed away; all are rotten with sin. Not one is good, not one!"

I never thought of myself as either bad or good, much less as righteous or evil, but those verses did touch a nerve. I knew that, as much as I tried, I was indeed absolutely incapable of being consistent in practicing even the universally accepted moral standards. Not only that but, speaking of "moral standards," I wondered where those standards came from in the first place?

Did we lie to one another just one too many times, hurting each other's feelings over and over again, and so one day we decided to make a moral law against lying? Were we at some moment in time unkind to each other so much that the pain was just too much to bear, so we decided that it should be morally imperative to do unto others as you would have them do unto you? Not likely. For, left to our own desires and whims, and to our ever present need for control and power, we would pay absolutely no heed to others. Power in this world comes from exactly the opposite values—sheer strength, cunning, deceit, ruthlessness, brutality. It may be nice to be nice, but not as nice as being powerful and in charge.

And then I remembered reading Immanuel Kant's

philosophical study Critique of Practical Reason, and being puzzled by one of his statements regarding morals. In it he writes: "Two things fill the mind with ever new and increasing admiration and awe... the starry heavens above me and the moral law within me." The moral law within me? At the time this truly puzzled me. But now I understood it all too clearly, and my mind filled with awe.

Whose standards are we trying to uphold if we endeavor to lead a "moral" life? Whose morals are the basis for the majority of human laws around the globe, if not our own? Whose moral law do I feel within me? The answer was unavoidable. Those morals are part of that power infinitely greater and older than we, whose righteousness we feel every time we sense guilt and shame, whose morality fills every pore of its creation, regardless of our unwillingness to acknowledge it. We breathe it in with our first breath, and with the second one we start viciously fighting it.

Throughout my atheist past, I certainly was neither willing nor capable of maintaining its ideals. Why deal with hurt feelings, or have to spend hours explaining the truth, or even worse, why risk an embarrassment, when one little white lie can fix it all? Immoral, yes... but practical, and so much less painful.

Why strain to be nice and considerate toward those in my class with lesser scholastic standing or slower academic progress, when just a few well-placed degrading remarks can make them look so much smaller and me so much bigger? Immoral, yes... but so empowering, and such a great shortcut to that much sought-after "smart and witty" reputation.

Why be modest and open-minded, allowing for the omnipotence of something greater than yourself, so evident even in a simple blade of grass? Why humbly allow the Creator of the universe to speak to you through His creation and His word, when you can be arrogantly proud of your own intellectual potential and power? Why go down the path that may lead to kneeling at the feet of Divinity in awe and veneration, when you can build altars to human wisdom, and, standing in their midst, be the one who is worshiped and adored. Immoral? Not according to my atheist heroes... but deadly just the same.

XXIII

BUT then, just as I was beginning to taste the reality of God's presence, the ideological ghosts of my past appeared out of nowhere, angrily trying to pull me back to their godless realm with the sheer weight of their thoughts. It is as if the whole history of my mind's path was projecting before me, like they say the life of a dying person appears before him, in fast-forward motion, moments before the last breath. Is this how an atheist mind draws its last breath?

Leading the parade was Friedrich Nietzsche, and his "liberating" opus—*Ecce Homo, Beyond Good and Evil, Thus Spoke Zarathustra, The Antichrist, The Genealogy of Morals,* and of course, the ever so lifting, *The Joyful Wisdom,* in which he asserts:

"The most important of more recent events—that God is dead, that the belief in the Christian God has become unworthy of belief—already begins to cast its first shadows over Europe... In fact, we philosophers and 'free spirits' feel ourselves irradiated as by a new dawn by the report that the old God is dead; our hearts overflow with gratitude, astonishment, presentiment and expectation. At last the horizon seems open once more, granting even that it is not bright; our ships can at last put out to sea in face of every danger; every hazard is again permitted to the discerner; the sea, our sea, again lies open before us; perhaps never before did such an open sea exist."

"No more God," he said, "God is dead." When I read this for the first time, as a high school student, it really didn't move me at all, for in my world God never existed. So this triumphant proclamation of His passing meant nothing at all, and I wondered at all the excitement. But what was reaffirming at the time was Nietzsche's assertion that man indeed creates his own meaning and path, that as much as we may feel otherwise, there was nothing absolute or predetermined about our values and morals. "We have become men," he writes in *Thus Spoke Zarathustra*, "so we want the kingdom of earth." Not the kingdom of heaven, but of earth, for God is dead and now we are free. Free from what, Friedrich? Apparently, free from sanity, for Nietzsche slowly but steadily lost his mental abilities, and died a lonely and angry madman.

Following at the heels of Nietzsche was German philosopher Ludwig Feuerbach, whose works did much damage to Christianity's reputation and swallowed plenty of young minds into its atheist depths. In his *The Essence of Christianity*, he writes:

"Man first of all sees his nature as if out of himself, before he finds it in himself. His own nature is in the first instance contemplated by him as that of another being... Hence the historical progress of religion consists in this: that what by an earlier religion was regarded as objective, is now recognized as subjective; that is, what was formerly contemplated and worshiped as God is now perceived to be something human."

Feuerbach contended that the idea of God was simply a projection of humanity's wants and desires. For him, God was a mirage, an illusion, the wishful thinking of hundreds of millions throughout centuries: a mass hallucination, from which, by the sheer brilliance of his mind, of course, he was thankfully spared, and thus emerged enlightened and free.

Right behind Feuerbach, impatiently waiting his turn, was one of the greatest heroes of the world I grew up in—Karl Marx. In *On Religion,* he taught us his views of God and His kingdom: "Man looked for the superman in the fantastic reality of heaven and found nothing there but the reflection of himself." Did I hear an "amen to that, brother" from Mr. Feuerbach? For his influence on Marx's ideas was obvious. Old Ludwig would have been more than pleased with this ideological disciple who went on to change the world and alter the eternity of immeasurable masses with his lethal elixir of atheism and political science.

I still remember the fervor with which my teachers spoke of Marx's ingenious mind, as a preface to the following quote from one of his manuscripts, which we had to analyze for a graded assignment:

"Man makes religion, religion does not make man. Religion is indeed man's self-consciousness and self-awareness as long as he has not found his feet in the universe. But man is not an abstract being, squatting outside the world. Man is the world of men, the State, and society. This State, this society, produces religion which is an inverted world consciousness, because they are an inverted world... Religious suffering is at the same time an expression of real suffering and a protest against real suffering. Religion is the sigh of the oppressed creature, the sentiment of a heartless world, and the soul of soulless conditions. It is the opium of the people. The abolition of religion, as the illusory happiness of men, is a demand for their real happiness."

Not only did Marx embrace Feuerbach's theory of the divine as an illusion, but he elevated religion to the status of a mortal enemy of man, "the opium of the people," a drug that stood in the way of our true happiness, and thus had to be abolished by any means necessary. How brilliant, to think that you can beat someone into "real happiness," even if it kills him. Just how much do you have to hate God and His people not only to believe something like that, but to actually create whole societies based on such an arrogant ideology?

Just behind Marx, in that ominous, ghostly procession stood Jean-Paul Sartre, one of my favorite youthful fascinations, the Nobel Prize winner, an existentialist philosopher of Nietzschean shade and bent. How many nights I spent reading and rereading his *Being and Nothingness,* desperately trying to unlock and soak in the mysteries of his thoughts. In it, he writes, "If God exists, man cannot be free. But man is free, therefore God cannot exist. Since God does not exist all things are morally permissible." Therefore, we are nothing but "an empty bubble on the sea of nothingness."

We are meaningless, the world is meaningless, the universe is meaningless. In the large scheme of things, it does not matter if we are born, if we live, or die. Sartre confirmed my worst atheist fears, and brought to life my darkest nightmares. Regardless of all the efforts to ascend higher, to reach further and deeper, the meaning of it all would surely elude me, for there was no meaning. So why live at all? I might as well end it all right now. "Yes, you can, if that's what you feel you should do," Sartre would say, "but just remember, it does not matter one way or the other." How motivating and uplifting, don't you think?

XXIV

AND so it went on, and on, and on. After Nietzsche, Feuerbach, Marx and Sartre, came Russell, Camus, Hume, Rousseau... All the apostles of atheism, whom I learned to worship throughout my socialist education, kept firing their arguments at me, relentlessly, almost frantically, like cornered animals fighting for their very lives. "What's wrong with you?" they shouted, "We taught you better than that. Can't you see that God is just an illusion, a fantasy of mass madness, a projection of humanity's wishful thinking? Isn't it obvious to you that His existence can't be scientifically proven, that we can see no evidence of His presence, and that therefore He does not exist? Don't you recognize that those poor, gullible souls who believe in Him are simply culturally conditioned into such a faith? Besides, if God made it all, who do you think made God? Can't you see that it all just happened on its own? Matter, time and chance... That's all there was, that's all there is. After all these years we spent with you, you can't possibly fall for the hoax of the 'Almighty Creator' and for the so-called 'divine truth.' There is no 'divine truth,' no absolute values, no absolute morals, no absolutes at all. For it's all relative."

Is that it? Is that the best they could come up with? Is this the chorus that kept me from knowing God all these years? Spiritual invalids, full of resentment, bitterness and hate? I couldn't believe it. It felt like awakening from a long, long sleep, like I was slowly coming to my senses from a forcefully induced mental paralysis, finally able to recognize not only the desperate nature of my past spiritual state, but also the shallowness and transparency of the atheistic intellectual alchemy. Somehow, now I could see straight through all of their arguments which had poisoned my mind ever since I could remember.

Faith in God as a projection of our wishful thinking? Even if true, how could I use that argument to disprove the existence of God? It only really addresses a possible scenario for the inception of faith, for the origin of the belief, not the object of faith itself. One cannot discredit the existence of God by simply explaining away how one came to believe.

God's existence cannot be scientifically proven? What if our science does not have appropriate tools, physical or intellectual, to measure or test such a thing as the "existence of God"? What if God is of a different substance than those testable by science? What if trying to prove God through science is like asking: "How loud is that ice-cream? Is that color blue salty at all?", I wondered. Nonsensical? Well, just as much as it is to try to prove God, or for that matter, love, passion, beauty, or devotion, through science.

The belief in God as a result of cultural and social conditioning? Surely even the most desperate atheists are not so foolish as to use such an argument. I couldn't believe that until now I simply accepted that claim at its face value. No questions asked. Talk about social conditioning. For it works both ways, you know. If I claimed that cultural or social conditioning played a crucial role in forming someone's belief in God, rendering it invalid, then I also had to admit an equal kind of influence on my own atheist belief, making it just as invalid.

If God made the world, then who made God? Now there is a curious argument, which I always thought was pretty convincing. But now it dawned on me—who said that God was made at all? Who said that everything must have a beginning, that absolutely everything must be made? Yes, in all our physical experiences we see that things have a beginning and an end, but God is not a thing.

God, with a capital G, is by definition eternal, infinite, with no beginning, and no end, the ultimate Creator. And besides, how is it that I allowed for the universe without a cause, an entirely self-created entity, but not for God without a cause? If absolutely nothing can be without a cause, then the universe has to have a cause, as well. But that might have led me to the Creator, as the logical next step, so my atheist mentors and teachers must have scrapped that idea as distasteful.

And how about the claim that it is all relative anyway? That there is no divine, absolute truth, and that each individual creates his or her own meaning and the ultimate path? Unless that path includes God, in which case all bets are off, right? It was painful to admit that it doesn't take much intellectual effort to realize that if truth is relative, then I should not complain about the believer's position at all. As a matter of fact, I should honor it. For, according to this claim, all theories are of equal validity, since it is all relative, and therefore, the believer's truth is at the very least just as true as my own atheist one.

This pondering of the question, "Is truth relative?" immediately reminded me of reading Plato's Dialogues, years before, in particularly *The Theaetetus*. But unlike in the past, where the conclusions of my reasoning were profoundly influenced by the narrow confines set by my atheist mentors, this time my reasoning led me to a decidedly different place. In *The Theaetetus*, Plato presents three propositions for examination: that knowledge is nothing but perception, that man is the measure of all things, and that absolutely everything is in flux, and therefore relative.

All three propositions stand closely related to each other, for if man is the measure of all things, he is the sole measure of his reality, measuring it with his senses, his perception, which in turn he deems as knowledge. Whatever appears to him is true for him as much as what appears to another is true for that person. And since one's perception not only differs from somebody else's perception, but also from one instance to another, the reality is therefore always changing, always in flux. See, everything is relative, just like my atheist mentors claimed, right? Well, let's see what Plato thinks.

It is true, Plato agrees, that there are different perceptions of things, and that we always truly perceive what we perceive, that there is no "misperception," and that therefore knowledge acquired through perception seems to be infallible. But is it the true knowledge? Does the true perception inevitably lead to the true knowledge?

If all men, individually, are the measure of all things, if what appears to be true to one is just as true as what appears to another, then why are we to consider any belief any more true than others, including the belief that everything is relative? Plato asks. What special claim to the nature of reality do the proponents of relativity have that others don't, if all is truly relative? None, of course. What we have here is not true knowledge, but simply an accumulation of separate perceptions as experienced by different individuals at different times, no one of them any closer to or farther from the truth than another, no one better or worse, but only different.

Plato contends that although it is true that things around us are changing, that they are indeed in flux, this is true only for physical, temporal things. For if absolutely everything is relative, and if each man is the sole measure of absolutely all things, then the knowledge of right and wrong, just and unjust, good and evil, would be unobtainable. It would be unobtainable because we would have no absolute standard on which to base our opinions. Right would not be right, and wrong would not be wrong; just would not be just, and unjust would not be unjust. There would be only different perceptions of different actions; there would only be history as the sum of all the past moments; there would only be different governments, and not better or worse; there would only be different people and characters, not wise or ignorant, good or bad, just or unjust.

Could I really believe that that's the true nature of reality? No universal standards that should serve as moral guides, for they cannot be discovered empirically? Appetites for power running rampant and wild, not checked by reason, but reinforced by appearances and perceptions? Justice rooted only in "nomos," in the customs and conventions of societies, and thus absolutely relative? Morality strictly based on individual opinions, and therefore even the term "good" left entirely without its meaning? Of course not. And neither could Plato.

For him, the acquisition of true knowledge is indeed possible, but only through "logos," through reason as the human phenomenon that orders perception, and reasoning that gives perception its true meaning. Yes, reasoning—like we are doing right now, and like I was doing alone in that room thousands of miles away from home, searching for the answer to the ultimate question, searching for God.

Knowledge may begin in perception, but it is ultimately acquired by reason free from the chains of appearances, Plato would argue. And it is that reason that led him to the recognition of the "Good" as the source of all true knowledge, as the one and the only Creator of it all. Not relative, not in flux; but eternal, and unchangeable; the one whose laws run through our veins, no matter how many intellectual transfusions we subject ourselves to.

Suddenly the text of Psalm 14:1 I read earlier rang loud and clear in my mind: "That man is a fool who says to himself, 'There is no God!'" And Plato was no fool. He may not have called it God, but the "Good" was good enough for me.

XXV

I REALIZED now that it took more blind faith to believe my atheist mentors than to believe in God. For as they categorically claimed and insisted that there is no God, they were really claiming that they indeed searched the whole universe, every infinite corner of it, and found it empty of Divinity. What they were really claiming was that they somehow communed with the inanimate cosmos, which in turn shared with them, confidentially of course, the secret of its inception and meaning, or the lack thereof.

In addition, by claiming with stubborn certainty that there is no God, they were claiming that they had the full and complete knowledge of reality and of all existence, not just here and now but throughout the universe, eternally. Doesn't that strangely remind you of something, or somebody? The All-knowing, The Ever-present, the Giver of knowledge... Oh, yes—God! To claim rightfully what they claimed, my atheist heroes had to become gods.

Ironic, isn't it? If they would have ever succeeded, they would have had to disprove themselves. Talk about faith. Could it get any more fantastic than that? How much more faith it required of me to believe that bizarre "logic" rather than the Creator God, the ultimate Mind behind this clockwork of the universe?

Yet the ideologues of atheism, my intellectual heroes, habitually and viciously attacked the faith of the believers while jealously guarding and hiding their own. Pure hypocrisy and contradiction. I realized then that it is only by pure faith that I believed in the universe without the divine cause and without the Creator, in morality without the absolutes, in values without the foundation, in life without the Giver of life. For atheism is indeed a religion—a godless one, but still a religion; a faith—blind, illogical, paradoxical, spiritless, but still a faith; a wide, comfortable path that leads to nowhere but depravity, depression, and the ultimate emptiness.

There is, indeed, an undeniable gaping hole in the center of every self-absorbed life, a hole that grows steadily wider, deeper and darker with every new day spent willfully and proudly denying the Maker, a hole that utterly destroys and devours all around it. Mine was so vast that only the infinite, almighty Creator could fill its terrifyingly dark and cold void. There was simply no denying His omnipotent existence any longer. The immense, painful chasm of separation He left inside me was indisputable.

For the first time in my life, I felt the need for His healing power and wisdom, and yet the weight of my sin seemed to have pulled me infinitely far away from

Him. How I wished I could turn back time, and make things right again.

I turned back to the Bible and found the next group of the verses as referenced on the bookmark—Romans 3:23-26, 5:8, 6:23; John 3:16; Ephesians 2:1-6:

"Yes, all have sinned; all fall short of God's glorious ideal; yet now God declares us `not guilty` of offending Him if we trust in Jesus Christ, who in His kindness freely takes away our sins. For God sent Christ Jesus to take our punishment for our sins and to end all God's anger against us. He used Christ's blood and our faith as the means of saving us from His wrath." (Romans 3:23-26)

"But God showed his great love for us by sending Christ to die for us while we were still sinners." (Romans 5:8)

"For the wages of sin is death, but the free gift of God is eternal life through Jesus Christ our Lord." (Romans 6:23)

"For God loved the world so much that he gave his only Son, so that anyone who believes in him shall not perish but have eternal life." (John 3:16)

"Once you were under God's curse, doomed forever for your sins. You went along with the crowd and were just like all the others, full of sin, obeying Satan, the mighty prince of the power of the air, who is at work right now in the hearts of those who are against the Lord. All of us used to be just as they are, our lives expressing the evil within us, doing every wicked thing that our passions or our evil thoughts might lead us into. We started out bad, being born with evil natures, and were under God's anger just like everyone else. But God is so rich in mercy; he loved us so much that even though we were spiritually dead and doomed by our sins, he gave us back our lives again when he raised Christ from the dead—only by his undeserved favor have we ever been saved—and lifted us up from the grave into glory along with Christ." (Ephesians 2:1-6)

I was beginning to suspect that there was a method to Mrs. Jean's list. (And indeed there was. As most evangelical Christians would recognize, it was a somewhat expanded version of the so-called "Roman Road" set of verses.) For just as I recognized the selfish, egotistical, and, above all, sinful nature of my own pride and arrogance, and just as the horror of living on the edge of eternal separation from the Creator was beginning to set in, the verses brought up God's love, mercy, and sacrifice, for each one of us... for me.

And not only at this moment, now that I was seeking Him with all of my heart, but even when I had still laughed at Him, when I still refused to believe in anything mightier than man, and ridiculed the faith and the faithful. Even then He had loved me, the Scriptures said, and in spite of my conceit and mockery, offered me His divine hand through the cross and the blood of Jesus. What an incredible, incredible thought—the Creator of the universe, the omnipotent Power, reaching out to me through the living Christ. But could my mind possibly accept such a claim as truth?

The academic nature of my past readings of the biblical texts, and all the careful intellectual maneuvering offered by my teachers and textbooks regarding this subject diverted my attention from the crucial point—that Christ died not for being "the King of the Jews," not for offending the Pharisees, not for enticing the riots... but for you and me. Because He wanted to. Because He loved us so. Because if humanity and divinity were to commune again, the price had to be paid for our sins, and we couldn't possibly afford its cost.

So He willingly took on the pain of the cross, and all the degrading burdens of humanity's sin onto His shoulders, and died a horrifying death. And as God raised Him into eternal life, He opened the gates of eternity and divine presence for all grave-bound sinners. His death was my life; His suffering, my blessing.

I couldn't see that truth before. For the view from the heights of human wisdom—which I had so enthusiastically climbed all of my life—is always obscured by the dark clouds of intellectual pride. This limited, obstructed view doesn't allow for relying on any power greater than our own.

But was simply knowing this enough to ensure my eternity with God? Would the divine peace somehow automatically come to me through my intellectual acknowledgement of His love and sacrifice? If that was the case, I worried that something was terribly wrong here, for my soul was still aflame.

No matter how clear my understanding of what God had done for me, no matter how many times I read those verses over and over, no matter how confident I was becoming in comprehending God's love, the fire inside me was still burning, and I felt bewildered by its persistence. There just had to be more to it than just an intellectual nod. Perhaps I needed to continue reading the Word.

XXVI

I PULLED out the bookmark, noted the next set of verses, and anxiously turned the pages in the Bible until the underlined text appeared.

"If you confess with your own mouth that Jesus Christ is your Lord, and believe in your own heart that God has raised him from the dead, you will be saved. For it is by believing in his heart that a man becomes right with God; and with his mouth he confesses his faith and is saved." (Romans 10:9-10)

"Anyone who calls upon the name of the Lord will be saved." (Romans 10:13)

No, it wasn't enough to just own the knowledge of the Truth. It had to be engraved onto my heart and confessed by my mouth. Straddling the fence was not, and is not, acceptable to God, and His Word was very clear about it. To be truly saved, to be right with God, my Creator, to cross that bridge from eternal separation from Him to His eternal embrace, I had to believe in my own heart and confess that belief with my own mouth. I had to believe Him, His Word, and Jesus, His Son, as the Lamb of God who took away the sins of the world, as my Savior and my Lord.

And there it was—the fork in the road. On one side was the very edge of the abyss of faith. To proceed toward Jesus, I had to jump off the familiar ground of academic surety and into the unknown depths of total and complete faith—the jump that transcended everything I had known before. On the other side of the fork was the wide, safe, easy and predictable, path of uninterrupted intellectualism, cautious skepticism, fashionable spiritualism, constant self-searches, and the never ending, yet ever-changing string of prudent and attractive gateways to "higher consciousness."

How could I possibly refuse the love of my Maker? How could I say "No" to an eternity in His gracious presence? How could I turn my back on finally becoming what each one of us is ultimately meant to be—a person who not only knows of God, but walks with Him as well? How could I not drink from the well of all wisdom and knowledge, of all love and beauty, of all goodness and mercy? His presence was too sweet, His call too inviting, His love too strong, His sacrifice too great, His mercy too gentle to refuse. I realized that, just as C. S. Lewis commented in one of his letters, I, too, was caught in the net of His grace, and there was no turning back.

But though I came so close to His truth that I could smell its intoxicating fragrance of freedom and joy all around me, there was one last question that haunted my mind. Is Christ the only answer, the only path, the only gate to salvation, the only door to God? Could I have not ended at the same spiritual destination through Buddha, Brahma, Muhammad, Confucius, or Lao Tse? Is He simply just one of the many roads leading upward to God, or is He the one, and the only, Savior? Bewildered, I looked down on the Bible lying open on my bed, and there, boldly underlined, was the last verse from Mrs. Jean's bookmark:

"Jesus answered, 'I am the way and the truth and the life. No one comes to the Father except through me.'" (John 14:6)

It's as if He heard my thoughts, and felt my bewilderment. It's as if He knew how desperately I needed the answer, so He mercifully granted it right there and then. Could His answer be any simpler and clearer? Certainly not. It left no room for discussion, no room for debate, no room for riding fences.

Finally, the atheist landscape of my socialist upbringing lay in ruins, and something new and sweet was springing up in its place. I slowly approached the edge of the only world I knew, closed my eyes and, with a prayer on my lips, let go and jumped into the unknown depths of faith. I chose to believe, to be born anew, to walk with my Creator.

With my own mouth, just as His Word said I should, I confessed my fallen nature and my sin, asked for His forgiveness and mercy, with my whole heart exalted Jesus, the Christ, His only Son. I asked that He come into my heart and be my Lord, too, my Savior, as unworthy as I was. And from that unforgettable moment on, I belonged to God, my heart transformed, my mind renewed forever, and I knew that nothing—absolutely nothing—could separate me from Him anymore.

In spite of the socialist world of my upbringing, in spite of all the diligent, atheist guardians of my mind and my heart, in spite of all the odds, God's grace was greater, and Christ came even into this heart, made it His own, and changed it forever. There is no presence more comforting, no knowledge more powerful, for there is no love and grace greater than His.

Through the power of prayer and God's amazing grace, through the power of His Holy Spirit, who took over my mind and gently led me through all the intellectual mazes and obstacles, through the power of the faithful witness of His people, who were not ashamed of the Gospel, who were more concerned about where am I going to spend eternity than what am I going to think of their intellects, even I came to know and live the Divine Truth.

Who would have ever thought that all the "somehows" that led me to America would also lead me to this extraordinary experience with the Divine? That in my search for excellence in this land of opportunity, I would encounter the Almighty God, the Creator

XXVI

A F E W weeks later, I auditioned for The Juilliard School, was admitted as a scholarship student and, after graduating, remained in New York, living and working in that great city for almost 15 years. My dream came true. But by then, God loomed so large in my life that I felt the power of yet another one of His miracles, of another "somehow"—somehow, that dream of studying at The Juilliard School and living in New York, or for that matter, any earthly dream, paled in comparison with His presence, His love and mercy. Somehow, by grace, I became His property, forgiven and saved, and the world just couldn't compete any more.

For, God is my Creator and my Master, Jesus my Savior and my Lord, Heaven my destiny and my home. Here, living and serving His truth, I'm just passing through. How about you?

THE JUILLIARD SCHOOL
PETER MENNIN, PRESIDENT
LINCOLN CENTER, NEW YORK, N. Y. 10023

OFFICE OF THE REGISTRAR

March 19, 1984

Darko Velichkovski
1606 Poplar Blvd.
Jackson, MS 39202

Dear Mr. Velichkovski,

I am happy to inform you that you have been admitted to The Juilliard School for the 1984-1985 academic year.

Further details regarding your program of study will be sent to you within two weeks. Since a thorough evaluation of your placement examination results and any previous study you have had must be made before your actual enrollment status can be determined, it is important for you to await these details before taking any further action. It is not possible at this time to guarantee acceptance in the program for which you applied.

Enclosed you will find general information concerning housing and financial matters. Other pertinent information will follow in the next mailing. If you have questions upon receipt of the second communication, please feel free to call for an appointment.

Congratulations and best wishes.

Darko's Juilliard acceptance letter, student ID, and (at 23 years old) graduating from The Juilliard School in New York City.

124

EPILOGUE

SINCE graduating from the Juilliard School, Darko has performed and toured extensively as a classical and jazz concert clarinetist, and has taught at a number of schools and universities as a faculty member and as a guest lecturer. During this period he has also earned his graduate degree in humanities at the City University of New York.

Since 1991, Darko has been professionally involved in the production and business aspects of the music industry, as well, taking on producing and engineering roles in projects of diverse musical genres. Subsequently, he formed Grace Productions Group, a music production company, which he still leads as President and Executive Producer.

In 1998, after 14 years of residing in New York City, Darko moved back to his spiritual birthplace—Jackson, Mississippi—where he took on the position of President and CEO of the Mississippi Symphony Orchestra. Three years later, led by a divine call to devote himself exclusively to Christian ministry, Darko resigned from all of his secular positions, transformed Grace Productions Group into a Christian music record label, and formed Grace

Ministries, a non-profit entity through which he carries most of his ministerial activities.

Ever since, Darko has been speaking and presenting programs of Christian testimony, inspiration and music across the U.S., as well as recording and producing Christian music.